Church of England

The Psalter, or, the Psalms of David

As Contained in the Authorised Version of the Holy Scriptures

Church of England

The Psalter, or, the Psalms of David
As Contained in the Authorised Version of the Holy Scriptures

ISBN/EAN:

Printed in Europe, USA, Canada, Australia, Japan

Cover: Foto ©Lupo / pixelio.de

More available books at **www.hansebooks.com**

Library of the Theological Seminary,
PRINCETON, N. J.

Shelf: Benson
Division: SCB
Section: 4341
Number:

The Psalter,

or

The Psalms of David,

as contained in

The Authorised Version of the Holy Scriptures.

MDCCCLXIII.

TABLE

OF THE PSALMS FOR

Morning and Evening Prayer,

FORENOON AND AFTERNOON SERVICES

AND

DAYS OF OBSERVANCE,

THROUGHOUT THE YEAR.

A Table of the Psalms

JANUARY, MARCH, MAY, JULY, SEPTEMBER, NOVEMBER.

Day.	Morning.	Forenoon.	Afternoon.	Evening.	Day.
1	i, ii.	lxxx.	lxxxi, lxxxii.	iii, iv.	1
2	v, vi.	lxxxiii.	lxxxiv.	vii, viii.	2
3	ix.	lxxxv.	lxxxvi, lxxxvii.	x.	3
4	xi, xii, xiii.	lxxxviii.	lxxxix. 1—18	xiv, xv, xvi.	4
5	xvii.	lxxxix. 19	xc.	xviii. 1—19	5
6	xviii. 20	xci.	xcii, xciii.	xix.	6
7	xx, xxi.	xciv.	xcv, xcvi.	xxii.	7
8	xxiii, xxiv.	xcvii, xcviii.	xcix, c, ci.	xxv.	8
9	xxvi, xxvii.	cii.	ciii.	xxviii, xxix.	9
10	xxx.	civ. 1—23	civ. 24	xxxi.	10
11	xxxii.	cv. 1—22	cv. 23	xxxiii.	11
12	xxxiv.	cvi. 1—33	cvi. 34	xxxv.	12
13	xxxvi.	cvii. 1—22	cvii. 23	xxxvii. 1—22	13
14	xxxvii. 23	cviii.	cix.	xxxviii.	14
15	xxxix.	cx, cxi, cxii.	cxiii, cxiv.	xl.	15
16	xli.	cxv.	cxvi, cxvii.	xlii, xliii.	16
17	xliv.	cxviii.	cxix. 1—16	xlv.	17
18	xlvi, xlvii.	cxix. 17—32	cxix. 33—48	xlviii.	18
19	xlix.	cxix. 49—64	cxix. 65—80	l.	19
20	li.	cxix. 81—96	cxix. 97—112	lii, liii, liv.	20
21	lv.	cxix. 113—128	cxix. 129—144	lvi.	21
22	lvii, lviii.	cxix. 145—160	cxix. 161	lix.	22
23	lx, lxi.	cxx, cxxi, cxxii.	cxxiii, cxxiv, cxxv.	lxii, lxiii.	23
24	lxiv, lxv.	cxxvi, cxxvii, cxxviii.	cxxix, cxxx, cxxxi.	lxvi.	24
25	lxvii, lxviii. 1-16	cxxxii, cxxxiii.	cxxxiv, cxxxv.	lxviii. 17	25
26	lxix. 1—19.	cxxxvi.	cxxxvii, cxxxviii.	lxix. 20, lxx.	26
27	lxxi.	cxxxix.	cxl.	lxxii.	27
28	lxxiii.	cxli, cxlii.	cxliii.	lxxiv.	28
29	lxxv, lxxvi.	cxliv.	cxlv.	lxxvii.	29
30	lxxviii. 1—31	cxlvi.	cxlvii.	lxxviii. 32—54.	30
31	lxxviii. 55	cxlviii.	cxlix, cl.	lxxix.	31

Proper Psalms for

	Morning.	Forenoon.	Afternoon.	Evening.
Christmas Eve	lxxx.	cxliii, cxliv.	cxxiii, cxxiv, cxxv.	lxxii.
Christmas Day	xc, xci.	lxxxiv, lxxxv.	cxxxii.	xlv.
Circumcision	xl.	cxvi, cxvii.	xxxvii.	ci.
Presentation in the Temple	cxvi.	xci, xcii.	cxviii.	xxvii.
Wednesday in Passion Week	cxix. 1—16	cxix. 17—40	cxix. 41—64	cxix. 65—88.

throughout the Year.

FEBRUARY, APRIL, JUNE, AUGUST, OCTOBER, DECEMBER.

Day.	Morning.	Forenoon.	Afternoon.	Evening.	Day.
1	lxxx.	i, ii.	iii, iv.	lxxxi, lxxxii.	1
2	lxxxiii.	v, vi.	vii, viii.	lxxxiv.	2
3	lxxxv.	ix.	x.	lxxxvi, lxxxvii.	3
4	lxxxviii.	xi, xii, xiii.	xiv, xv, xvi.	lxxxix. 1—18	4
5	lxxxix. 19	xvii.	xviii. 1—19	xc.	5
6	xci.	xviii. 20	xix.	xcii, xciii.	6
7	xciv.	xx, xxi.	xxii.	xcv, xcvi.	7
8	xcvii, xcviii.	xxiii, xxiv.	xxv.	xcix, c, ci.	8
9	cii.	xxvi, xxvii.	xxviii. xxix.	ciii.	9
10	civ. 1—23	xxx.	xxxi.	civ. 24	10
11	cv. 1—22	xxxii.	xxxiii.	cv. 23	11
12	cvi. 1—33	xxxiv.	xxxv. 1—18	cvi. 34	12
13	cvii. 1—22	xxxv. 19, xxxvi.	xxxvii. 1—22	cvii. 23	13
14	cviii.	xxxvii. 23	xxxviii.	cix.	14
15	cx, cxi, cxii.	xxxix.	xl.	cxiii, cxiv.	15
16	cxv.	xli.	xlii, xliii.	cxvi, cxvii.	16
17	cxviii.	xliv.	xlv.	cxix. 1—16	17
18	cxix. 17—32	xlvi, xlvii.	xlviii.	cxix. 33—48	18
19	cxix. 49—64	xlix.	l.	cxix. 65—80	19
20	cxix. 81—96	li.	lii, liii, liv.	cxix. 97—112	20
21	cxix. 113—128	lv.	lvi.	cxix. 129—144	21
22	cxix. 145—160	lvii, lviii.	lix.	cxix. 161	22
23	cxx, cxxi, cxxii.	lx, lxi.	lxii, lxiii.	cxxiii, cxxiv, cxxv.	23
24	cxxvi, cxxvii, cxxviii.	lxiv, lxv.	lxvi.	cxxix, cxxx, cxxxi.	24
25	cxxxii, cxxxiii.	lxvii, lxviii. 1-16	lxviii. 17	cxxxiv, cxxxv.	25
26	cxxxvi.	lxix. 1—19	lxix. 20, lxx.	cxxxvii, cxxxviii.	26
27	cxxxix.	lxxi.	lxxii.	cxl.	27
28	cxli, cxlii.	lxxiii.	lxxiv.	cxliii.	28
29	cxliv.	lxxv, lxxvi.	lxxvii.	cxlv.	29
30	cxlvi.	lxxviii. 1—31	lxxviii. 32—54.	cxlvii.	30
31	cxlviii.	lxxviii. 55	lxxix.	cxlix. cl.	31

Days of Observance.

	Morning.	Forenoon.	Afternoon.	Evening.
Thursday in Passion Week	cxix. 89—104	cxix. 105—128	cxix. 129—152	cxix. 153
Good Friday	li.		lxxxviii, cxlii.	cxl, cxli.
Easter Eve	c.	xxvii, xxviii.	xxx, xxxi.	xv, xvi.
Easter Day	cx, cxi.	lxxii.	cxviii.	cxiii, cxiv.
Ascension	xx, xxi.	xlv, xlvii.	cxviii.	xxiv, xxvii.
Pentecost	xlviii.	lxviii.	civ.	cxlv.
All Angels	ciii.	civ.	cxlviii, cxlix.	viii, xci.
All Saints	xlv.	lxxii.	xvi, cxviii.	xlvii, xlviii.

Thomas Laurie, 92 Prince's Street, Edinburgh.

THE PSALMS.

PSALM I.

BLESSED is the man that walketh not in the coun-sel' of the‿un-godly,
    Nor standeth in the way of sinners, nor sitteth in the' sëat of the scornful.
2 But his delight is in the' law of the‿Lord;
    And in his law doth he' medi-tate day and night.
3 And he shall be like a tree planted by the rivers of water, that bringeth forth his' fruit in his season;
    His leaf also shall not wither; and whatso'ever he doeth shall prosper.
4 The ungodly' are not so:
    But are like the chaff' which the‿wind driveth a-way.
5 Therefore the ungodly shall not' stand in the‿judg-ment,
    Nor sinners in the congre'ga-tion of the righteous.
6 For the LORD knoweth the' way of the‿righteous:
    But the way' of the‿un-godly shall perish.

PSALM II.

WHY do the' hea-then rage,
    And the people i'magine a väin thing?
2 The kings of the earth set themselves, and the rulers take' counsel to-gether,
    Against the LORD, and a'gäinst his An-ointed,
3 Saying, Let us break their' bands a-sunder,
    And cast a'way their cörds from‿us.

PSALMS.

4 He that sitteth in the' heavens shall laugh:
    The LORD shall' have them in de-rision.
5 Then shall he speak unto them' in his wrath,
    And vex them' in his sore dis-pleasure.
6 Yet have I' set my king
    Upon my' ho-ly hill of Zion.
7 I will declare the decree: the LORD hath' said un-to me,
    Thou art my Son; this' day have I be-gotten_thee.
8 Ask of me, and I shall give thee the heathen for' thine in-heritance,
    And the uttermost parts of the' earth for thy pos-session.
9 Thou shalt break them with a' rod of iron;
    Thou shalt dash them in pieces' like a pot-ter's vessel.
10 Be wise now, therefore', O ye kings:
    Be instructed, ye' jud-ges of the earth.
11 Serve the' LORD with fear,
    And re'jö'ice with trembling.
12 Kiss the Son, lest he be angry, and ye perish from the way, when his wrath is kindled' but a little.
    Blessed are all they that' put their trust in him.

PSALM III.

¶ A Psalm of David, when he fled from Absalom his son.

LORD, how are they in'creased that trouble_me?
    Many are they' that rise up a-gainst_me.
2 Many there be which say' of my soul,
    There is no' help for him in God. Selah.
3 But thou, O LORD, art a' shield for me;
    My glory, and the' lifter up of mine head.
4 I cried unto the LORD' with my voice,
    And he heard me' out of_his ho-ly hill. Selah.
5 I laid me' down and slept;
    I awaked'; for the Lord sus-tained_me.

6 I will not be afraid of ten' thousands of people,
That have set themselves a'gainst me round a-bout.
7 Arise, O Lord; save me', O my God:
For thou hast smitten all mine enemies upon the cheek-bone; thou hast broken the' teeth of the un-godly.
8 Salvation belongeth' unto the Lord:
Thy blessing' is up-on thy people. Selah.

PSALM IV.

¶ To the chief Musician on Neginoth. A Psalm of David.

HEAR me when I call, O God' of my righteousness;
Thou hast enlarged me when I was in distress;
have mercy upon' me and hear my prayer.
2 O ye sons of men, how long will ye turn my' glory into shame?
How long will ye love vanity, and' seek af-ter leasing? Selah.
3 But know that the Lord hath set apart him that is godly' for him-self:
The Lord will hear' when I call un-to him.
4 Stand in' awe, and sin not:
Commune with your own heart upon your' bed, and be still. Selah.
5 Offer the sacri'fices of righteousness,
And' put your trust in the Lord.
6 There be many that say, Who will show us' a-ny good?
Lord, lift thou up the light' of thy countenance up-on us.
7 Thou hast put gladness' in my heart,
More than in the time that their' corn and their wine in-creased.
8 I will both lay me down in' peace, and sleep:
For thou, Lord, only' makest me dwell in safety.

PSALMS.

PSALM V.

¶ To the chief Musician upon Nehiloth. A Psalm of David.

GIVE ear to my' words, O Lord;
Con'sider my me-di-tation.
2 Hearken unto the voice of my cry, my King', and my God:
For' unto thee will I pray.
3 My voice shalt thou hear in the' morning, O Lord;
In the morning will I direct my prayer unto' thee, and will look up.
4 For thou art not a God that hath' pleasure in wickedness:
Neither shall' e-vil dwell with thee.
5 The foolish shall not' stand in‿thy sight:
Thou hatest all' work-ers of i-niquity.
6 Thou shalt destroy them' that speak leasing:
The LORD will abhor the' bloody and deceit-ful man.
7 But as for me, I will come into thy house in the multitude' of thy mercy:
And in thy fear will I worship' toward thy ho-ly temple.
8 Lead me, O LORD, in thy righteousness, because' of mine enemies;
Make thy way' straight be-fore my face.
9 For there is no faithfulness in their mouth; their inward part is' ve-ry wickedness;
Their throat is an open sepulchre; they' flat-ter with their tongue.
10 Destroy thou them, O God; let them fall by their' öwn counsels;
Cast them out in the multitude of their transgressions: for they' have re-belled a-gainst‿thee.
11 But let all those that put their trust in' thee re-joice:
Let them ever shout for joy, because thou defendest them: let them also that love thy' name be joyful in thee.

PSALMS.

12 For thou, LORD, wilt' bless the righteous;
  With favours wilt thou' compass him as with‿a shield.

PSALM VI.

¶ To the chief Musician on Neginoth upon Sheminith.
A Psalm of David.

O LORD, rebuke me not' in thine anger,
  Neither chasten me' in thy hot dis-pleasure.
2 Have mercy upon me, O LORD; for' I am weak:
  O LORD, heal me'; for my bones are vexed.
3 My soul is' also sore vexed:
  But' thou, O LORD, how long?
4 Return, O LORD, de'liver my soul.
  O save me' for thy mer-cies' sake.
5 For in death there is no re'membrance of thee;
  In the grave' who shall give thee thanks?
6 I am weary' with my groaning;
  All the night make I my bed to swim; I water my' cöuch with my tears.
7 Mine eye is consumed be'cause of grief;
  It waxeth old be'cause of all mine enemies.
8 Depart from me, all ye workers' of i-niquity;
  For the LORD hath heard the' vöice of my weeping.
9 The LORD hath heard my' sup-pli-cation;
  The LORD' will re-ceive my prayer.
10 Let all mine enemies be ashamed and' söre vexed:
  Let them return and' be a-sham-ed suddenly.

PSALM VII.

¶ Shiggaion of David, which he sang unto the LORD, concerning the words of Cush the Benjamite.

O LORD my God, in thee do I' put my trust:
  Save me from all them that' persecute me, and de-liver‿me:

PSALMS.

2 Lest he tear my' soul like a lion,
  Rending it in pieces, while there is' nöne to de-liver.
3 O Lord my God, if I' have done this;
  If there be i'niqui-ty in my hands;
4 If I have rewarded evil unto him that was at' peace with me;
  (Yea, I have delivered him that with'out cause is mine enemy:)
5 Let the enemy persecute my' soul, and take it;
  Yea, let him tread down my life upon the earth, and' lay mine honour in the dust. Selah.
6 Arise, O Lord, in thine anger, lift up thyself because of the rage' of mine enemies:
  And awake for me to the judgment' that thou hast com-manded.
7 So shall the congregation of the people compass' thee a-bout;
  For their sakes, therefore, re'türn thou on high.
8 The Lord shall' judge the people:
  Judge me, O Lord, according to my righteousness, and according to mine in'tegri-ty that is in me.
9 Oh let the wickedness of the wicked come to an end; but es'tablish the just:
  For the righteous God' trieth the hearts and reins.
10 My defence' is of God,
  Which' saveth the upright in heart.
11 God' judgeth the righteous,
  And God is angry with the' wick-ed ev-ery day.
12 If he turn not, he will' whet his sword;
  He hath bent his' bow, and made it ready.
13 He hath also prepared for him the' instruments of death;
  He ordaineth his' arrows a-gainst the persecutors.
14 Behold he travaileth' with i-niquity,
  And hath conceived' mischief, and brought forth falsehood.

15 He made a' pit, and digged it,
And is fallen in'to the‿ditch which he made.
16 His mischief shall return upon' his own head,
And his violent dealing shall come' down upon his own pate.
17 I will praise the LORD according' to his righteousness:
And will sing praise to the' name of the‿Lord most high.

PSALM VIII.

¶ To the chief Musician upon Gittith. A Psalm of David.

O LORD our Lord, how excellent is thy name in' all the earth!
Who hast set thy' glory a-bove the heavens.
2 Out of the mouth of babes and sucklings hast thou ordained strength because' of thine enemies,
That thou mightest still the' enemy and the a-venger.
3 When I consider thy heavens, the work' of thy fingers,
The moon and the stars', which thou hast or-dained;
4 What is man, that thou art' mindful of him?
And the son of man', that thou visit-est him?
5 For thou hast made him a little' lower than the‿angels,
And hast crowned' him with glory and honour.
6 Thou madest him to have dominion over the works' of thy hands;
Thou hast put' all things under his feet.
7 All' sheep and oxen,
Yea, and the' beasts of the field;
8 The fowl of the air, and the' fish of the‿sea,
And whatsoever passeth' through the paths of the‿seas.
9 O' Lord our Lord,
How excellent is thy' name in all the earth!

PSALMS.

PSALM IX.

¶ To the chief Musician upon Muth-labben. A Psalm of David.

1 WILL praise thee, O LORD, with my' whöle heart;
I will show forth' all thy marvel-lous works.
2 I will be glad and re'joice in thee:
I will sing praise to thy' name, O thou most High.
3 When mine enemies are' turn-ed back,
They shall fall and' per-ish at thy presence.
4 For thou hast maintained my right' and my cause;
Thou satest in the' thröne judg-ing right.
5 Thou hast rebuked the heathen, thou hast de'stroy-ed the wicked,
Thou hast put out their' name for ever and ever.
6 O thou enemy, destructions are come to a per'-pet-ual end;
And thou hast destroyed cities; their me'morial is perish-ed with_them.
7 But the LORD shall en'dure for ever:
He hath pre'pared his throne for judgment.
8 And he shall judge the' world in righteousness,
He shall minister judgment to the' peo-ple in up-rightness.
9 The LORD also will be a refuge' for the_op-pressed,
A' refuge in times of trouble.
10 And they that know thy name will put their' trust in thee:
For thou, LORD, hast not for'sak-en them that seek_thee.
11 Sing praises to the LORD, which' dwelleth in Zion;
Declare a'mong the people his doings.
12 When he maketh inquisition for blood', he re-mem-bereth_them:
He forgetteth' not the cry of the_humble.
13 Have mercy upon me, O LORD; consider my trouble which I suffer of' them that hate_me,
Thou that liftest me up' from the gates of death:

PSALMS.

14 That I may show forth all thy praise in the gates of the' daughter of Zion:
I will re'joice in thy sal-vation.
15 The heathen are sunk down in the pit' that they made:
In the net which they hid' is their own foot taken.
16 The LORD is known by the judgment' which he executeth:
The wicked is snared in the' work of his own hands. Higgaion. Selah.
17 The wicked shall be turned' in-to hell,
And all the nations' that for-gët God.
18 For the needy shall not alway' be for-gotten:
The expectation of the poor' shall not perish for ever.
19 Arise, O LORD; let not' man pre-vail:
Let the heathen be' judg-ed in thy sight.
20 Put them in' fear, O Lord:
That the nations may know them'selves to be but men. Selah.

PSALM X.

WHY standest thou afar' off, O Lord?
Why hidest thou thy'self in times of trouble?
2 The wicked in his pride doth' persecute the poor:
Let them be taken in the devices' that they have i-magined.
3 For the wicked boasteth of his' heart's de-sire,
And blesseth the covetous', whom the Lord ab-hor-reth.
4 The wicked, through the pride of his countenance, will not' seek after God:
God is' not in all his thoughts.
5 His ways are always grievous; thy judgments are far above', out‿of his sight:
As for all his' enemies, he puff-eth at‿them.

PSALMS.

6 He hath said in his heart I shall' not be moved:
For I shall' never be in ad-versity.
7 His mouth is full of cursing and de'ceit and fraud:
Under his' tongue is mischief and vanity.
8 He sitteth in the lurking' places of the villages:
In the secret places doth he murder the innocent:
his eyes are privily' set a-gainst the poor.
9 He lieth in wait secretly as a lion in his den; he lieth in wait to' catch the poor:
He doth catch the poor when he' draweth him into his net.
10 He croucheth, and' humbleth him-self,
That the poor may' fäll by his strong ones.
11 He hath said in his heart, God' hath for-gotten:
He hideth his face'; he will ne-ver see it.
12 Arise, O LORD; O God, lift' up thine hand:
Fo'r-gët not the humble.
13 Wherefore doth the wicked con'tëmn God?
He hath said in his heart', thou wilt not re-quire it.
14 Thou hast seen it; for thou beholdest mischief and spite, to requite it' with thy hand:
The poor committeth himself unto thee; thou art the' help-er of the fatherless.
15 Break thou the arm of the wicked and the' e-vil man :
Seek out his wickedness' till thou find none.
16 The LORD is King for' ever and ever:
The heathen are' perished out of his land.
17 LORD, thou hast heard the de'sire of the humble:
Thou wilt prepare their heart, thou wilt' cause thine ear to hear.
18 To judge the fatherless' and the op-pressed,
That the man of the earth' may no more op-press.

PSALMS.

PSALM XI.

¶ To the Chief Musician. A Psalm of David.

IN the Lord put' I my trust:
How say ye to my soul, Flee as a' bird to your mountain?
2 For, lo, the wicked bend their bow, they make ready their arrow up'on the string,
That they may privily' shoot at the‿upright in heart.
3 If the foundations' be de-stroyed,
What' can the right-eous do?
4 The Lord is in his holy temple, the Lord's' throne is‿in heaven:
His eyes behold, His eyelids' try the children of men.
5 The Lord' trieth the righteous:
But the wicked and him that loveth' violence his söul hateth.
6 Upon the wicked he shall rain snares, fire and brimstone, and an' horri-ble tempest:
This shall be the' por-tion of their cup.
7 For the righteous Lord' lov-eth righteousness;
His countenance' doth be-hold the upright.

PSALM XII.

¶ To the chief Musician upon Sheminith. A Psalm of David.

HELP, Lord; for the' godly man ceaseth;
For the faithful fail from a'mong the children of men.
2 They speak vanity every one' with his neighbour:
With flattering lips and with a' double heart do they speak.
3 The Lord shall cut off all' flatter-ing lips,
And the' tongue that speaketh proud things,
4 Who have said, With our tongue will' we pre-vail;
Our lips are our own': who is lord over us?

PSALMS.

5 For the oppression of the poor, for the sighing of the needy, now will I arise', saith the LORD;
I will set him in safety from' him that puff-eth at him.
6 The words of the LORD are' püre words:
As silver tried in a furnace of earth' puri-fied se-ven times.
7 Thou shalt keep' them, O LORD,
Thou shalt preserve them from' this gene-ration for ever.
8 The wicked walk on' e-very side,
When the' vilest men are ex-alted.

PSALM XIII.

¶ To the chief Musician. A Psalm of David.

HOW long wilt thou forget me, O' LORD? for ever?
How long wilt thou' hide thy fäce from me?
2 How long shall I take counsel in my soul, having sorrow in my' hëart daily?
How long shall mine enemy' be ex-alt-ed over me?
3 Consider and hear me, O' LORD my God:
Lighten mine eyes, lest I' sleep the sleep of death;
4 Lest mine enemy say, I have pre'vailed a-gainst him;
And those that trouble me re'joice when I am moved.
5 But I have trusted' in thy mercy;
My heart shall re'joice in thy sal-vation. '
6 I will sing un'to the LORD,
Because he' hath dealt bounti-fully with me.

PSALM XIV.

¶ To the chief Musician. A Psalm of David.

THE fool hath said in his heart, There is' nö God.
They are corrupt, they have done abominable works, there is' none that do-eth good.

PSALMS.

2 The LORD looked down from heaven upon the'
children of men,
To see if there were any that did under'stand and
sëek God.
3 They are all gone aside, they are all together be'-
cöme filthy:
There is none that doeth' göod, no, not one.
4 Have all the workers of i'niquity no knowledge?
Who eat up my people as they eat bread, and'
call not up-on the LORD.
5 There were they' in great fear:
For God is in the gene'ra-tion of the righteous.
6 Ye have shamed the' counsel of the poor,
Because the' LÖRD is his refuge.
7 O that the salvation of Israel were come' out of
Zion!
When the LORD bringeth back the captivity of his
people, Jacob shall rejoice, and' Is-rael shall be
glad.

PSALM XV.

¶ A Psalm of David.

LORD, who shall abide' in thy tabernacle?
Who shall dwell' in thy ho-ly hill?
2 He that walketh uprightly, and' work-eth righteousness,
And speaketh the' trüth in his heart.
3 He that backbiteth not' with his tongue,
Nor doeth evil to his neighbour, nor taketh up a
re'proach a-gainst his neighbour.
4 In whose ëyes a vile person is contemned; but he
honoureth them that' fear the LORD.
He that sweareth to his own' hurt, and chang-eth
not.
5 He that putteth not out his money to usury, nor
taketh reward a'gainst the innocent.
He that doeth these' things shall never be moved.

PSALMS.

PSALM XVI.

¶ Michtam of David.

PRESERVE' me, O God:
    For in thee' do I put my trust.
2 O my soul, thou hast said unto the Lord, Thou' art my Lord:
My goodness ex'tend-eth not to thee:
3 But to the saints that are' in the earth,
And to the excellent, in whom' is all my de-light.
4 Their sorrows shall be multiplied that hasten after an'o-ther god:
Their drink-offerings of blood will I not offer, nor take up their' names in-to my lips.
5 The Lord is the portion of mine inheritance, and' of my cup:
Thou main'täin-est my lot.
6 The lines are fallen unto me in' plea-sant places:
Yea, I' have a good-ly heritage.
7 I will bless the Lord, who hath' given me counsel:
My reins also in'struct me in the night seasons.
8 I have set the Lord' always be-fore me:
Because he is at my right hand', I shall not be moved.
9 Therefore my heart is glad, and my' glory re-joiceth:
My flesh' also shall rest in hope.
10 For thou wilt not leave my' soul in hell:
Neither wilt thou suffer thine' Holy One to see cor-ruption.
11 Thou wilt show me the' path of life:
In thy presence is fulness of joy; at thy right hand there are' pleasures for ev-er-more.

PSALMS.

PSALM XVII.

¶ A Prayer of David.

HEAR the right, O LORD, attend un'to my cry,
Give ear unto my prayer, that goeth not' out of feign-ed lips.
2 Let my sentence come forth' from thy presence;
Let thine eyes be'hold the‿things that are equal.
3 Thou hast proved mine heart; thou hast visited me in the night; thou hast tried me, and' shalt find nothing;
I am purposed that my' mouth shall not trans-gress.
4 Concerning the' works of men,
By the word of thy lips I have kept me from the' paths of the de-stroyer.
5 Hold up my goings' in thy paths,
That' my foot-steps slip not.
6 I have called upon thee, for thou wilt' hear‿me, O God:
Incline thine ear unto' me, and hear my speech.
7 Show thy marvellous loving-kindness, O thou that savest by thy right hand them which put their' trust in thee
From those that' rise up a-gainst‿them.
8 Keep me as the' apple of the‿eye,
Hide me under the' sha-dow of thy wings,
9 From the wicked' that op-press‿me,
From my deadly enemies who' com-pass me a-bout.
10 They are inclosed in their' öwn fat:
With their' mouth they spëak proudly.
11 They have now compassed us' in our steps:
They have set their eyes' bowing down to the earth;
12 Like as a lion that is greedy' of his prey,
And as it were a young lion' lurking in se-cret places.
13 Arise, O LORD, disappoint him', cast him down:
Deliver my soul from the' wicked, which is thy sword;

15

PSALMS.

14 From men which are thy hand, O Lord, from men of the world, which have their portion in this life, and whose belly thou fillest with' thy hid treasure:
They are full of children, and leave the rest of their' sub-stance to their babes.
15 As for me, I will behold thy' face in righteousness: I shall be satisfied, when I a'wäke with thy likeness.

PSALM XVIII.

¶ To the chief Musician. A Psalm of David.

I' WILL love thee,
O' Lörd, my strength.
2 The Lord is my rock, and my fortress and' my de-liverer;
My God, my strength, in whom I will trust; my buckler, and the horn of my sal'vation, and my high tower.
3 I will call upon the Lord, who is worthy' to be praised:
So shall I be' sav-ed from mine enemies.
4 The sorrows of death' compass-ed me,
And the floods of ungodly' men made me a-fraid.
5 The sorrows of hell compassed' me a-bout:
The snares of' death pre-vent-ed me.
6 In my distress I called upon the Lord, and cried un'to my God:
He heard my voice out of his temple, and my cry came before him', ev-en into his ears.
7 Then the earth' shook and trembled;
The foundations also of the hills moved and were shaken, be'caüse he was wroth.
8 There went up a smoke out of his nostrils, and fire out of his' mouth de-voured:
Co'äls were kin-dled by it.
9 He bowed the heavens also', and cäme down:
And' darkness was under his feet.

PSALMS.

10 And he rode upon a cherub′, and did fly:
   Yea, he did fly up′on the wings of the‿wind.
11 He made darkness his′ se-cret place;
   His pavilion round about him were dark waters and′ thick clouds of the‿skies.
12 At the brightness that was before him his′ thick clouds passed:
   Hail′stones and coals of fire.
13 The LORD also thundered′ in the heavens,
   And the Highest gave his voice; hail′stones and coals of fire.
14 Yea, he sent out his′ arrows, and scattered‿them;
   And he shot out′ light-nings, and dis-comfited‿them.
15 Then the channels of waters were seen, and the foundations of the world′ were dis-covered
   At thy rebuke, O LORD, at the blast of the′ brëath of thy nostrils.
16 He sent from a′bove, he took‿me,
   He drew me′ out of ma-ny waters.
17 He delivered me from my strong enemy, and from′ them which hated‿me:
   For′ they were too strong for‿me.
18 They prevented me in the day of′ my ca-lamity:
   But the′ LÖRD was my stay.
19 He brought me forth also into a′ lärge place;
   He delivered me′, because he delight-ed in‿me.
20 The LORD rewarded me according′ to my right-eousness;
   According to the cleanness of my hands′ hath he recom-pensed me.
21 For I have kept the′ ways of the‿LORD,
   And have not wickedly de′part-ed from my God.]′
22 For all his judgments′ were be-fore‿me,
   And I did not put a′way his sta-tutes from‿me.
23 I was also′ upright be-fore‿him,
   And I kept my′self from mine i-niquity.
24 Therefore hath the LORD recompensed me accord-ing′ to my righteousness,

B   .   17

PSALMS.

According to the cleanness of my' händs in his eyesight.
25 With the merciful thou wilt' show thyself merciful;
With an upright man' thou wilt show‿thyself upright;
26 With the pure thou wilt' show thyself pure:
And with the froward' thou wilt show thyself froward.
27 For thou wilt save the af'flict-ed people;
But' wilt bring down high looks.
28 For thou wilt' light my candle:
The LORD my God' will en-lighten my darkness.
29 For by thee I have' run through a‿troop;
And by my God have I' leap-ed over a wall.
30 As for God, his' way is perfect:
The word of the LORD is tried, he is a buckler to all' those that trust in him.
31 For who is God' save the LORD?
Or who' is‿a rock save our God?
32 It is God that girdeth' me with strength,
And' mak-eth my way perfect.
33 He maketh my' feet like hinds'‿feet,
And setteth' me upon my high places.
34 He teacheth my' hands to war,
So that a bow of steel is' brok-en by mine arms.
35 Thou hast also given me the shield of' thy sal-vation:
And thy right hand hath holden me up, and thy' gentleness hath made me great.
36 Thou hast enlarged my' stëps under‿me,
That' my feet did not slip.
37 I have pursued mine enemies, and' o-ver-taken‿them:
Neither did I turn again' till they were con-sumed.
38 I have wounded them that they were not' able to rise:
They are' fall-en under my feet.
39 For thou hast girded me with strength' unto the battle:
Thou hast subdued under me those that' röse up a-gainst‿me.

18

PSALMS.

40 Thou hast also given me the necks' of mine enemies,
   That I' might destroy them that hate‿me.
41 They cried, but there was' none to save‿them:
   Even unto the LORD', but he answered them not.
42 Then did I beat them small as the dust be'fore the wind:
   I did cast them out' as the dirt in the‿streets.
43 Thou hast delivered me from the strivings of the people; and thou hast made me the' head of the‿heathen:
   A people whom I' have not known shall serve‿me.
44 As soon as they hear of me, they' shall o-bey‿me:
   The strangers shall sub'mit them-selves un-to‿me.
45 The strangers shall' fade a-way,
   And be afraid' out of their close places.
46 The LORD liveth; and blessed' be my rock;
   And let the God of my sal'va-tion be ex-alted.
47 It is God that a'ven-geth me,
   And sub'dueth the people un-to‿me.
48 He delivereth me from mine enemies: yea, thou lift-est me up above those that rise' up a-gainst‿me:
   Thou hast delivered me' from the vio-lent man.
49 Therefore will I give thanks unto thee, O LORD, a'mong the heathen,
   And sing' praises un-to thy name.
50 Great deliverance giveth he' to his king;
   And showeth mercy to his anointed, to David, and to his' seed for ev-er-more.

PSALM XIX.

¶ To the chief Musician. A Psalm of David.

THE heavens declare the' glory of God;
   And the' fir-mament showeth his handywork.
2 Day unto day' utter-eth speech,
   And night' unto night show-eth knowledge.

PSALMS.

3 There is no' speech nor language,
Where their' vöice is not heard.
4 Their line is gone out through all the earth, and their words to the' end of the world.
In them hath he set a' taber-nacle for the sun,
5 Which is as a bridegroom coming' out of his chamber,
And rejoiceth as a strong' man to run a race.
6 His going forth is from the end of the heaven, and his circuit unto the' ends of it:
And there is nothing' hid from the heat there-of.
7 The law of the LORD is perfect, con'verting the soul:
The testimony of the LORD is sure', mak-ing wise the simple:
8 The statutes of the LORD are right, re'joicing the heart;
The commandment of the LORD is' pure, en-lightening the eyes:
9 The fear of the LORD is clean, en'during for ever:
The judgments of the LORD are true and' righteous al-to-gether.
10 More to be desired are they than gold, yea, than' much fine gold:
Sweeter also than' ho-ney and the honeycomb.
11 Moreover, by them is thy' ser-vant warned:
And in keeping of them' there is great re-ward.
12 Who can under'stand his errors?
Cleanse thou' me from se-cret faults.
13 Keep back thy servant also from presumptuous sins: let them not have do'min-ion over me:
Then shall I be upright, and I shall be innocent' from the great trans-gression.
14 Let the words of my mouth, and the meditation' of my heart,
Be acceptable in thy sight, O LORD, my' strength and my re-deemer.

PSALMS.

PSALM XX.

¶ To the chief Musician. A Psalm of David.

THE LORD hear thee in the' day of trouble;
    The name of the' God of Jacob de-fend_thee.
2 Send thee help' from the sanctuary,
    And' strengthen thee out of Zion.
3 Remember' all thy offerings,
    And ac'cept thy bürnt sacrifice. Selah.
4 Grant thee according to' thine own heart,
    And ful'fil äll thy counsel.
5 We will rejoice in thy salvation, and in the name
    of our God we will set' up our banners:
    The LORD ful'fil all thy pe-titions.
6 Now know I that the LORD saveth' his a-nointed:
    He will hear him from his holy heaven with the
    saving' strength of his right hand.
7 Some trust in chariots, and' some in horses:
    But we will remember the' name of the_LORD our
    God.
8 They are brought' down and fallen:
    But we are' risen, and stand up-right.
9 S'äve, LORD:
    Let the king' hear us when we call.

PSALM XXI.

¶ To the chief Musician. A Psalm of David.

THE king shall joy in thy' strength, O LORD;
    And in thy salvation how' greatly shall he
    re-joice!
2 Thou hast given him his' heart's de-sire,
    And hast not withholden the re'quëst of his lips.
    Selah.
3 For thou preventest him with the' blessings of
    goodness;
    Thou settest a crown of' pure gold on his head.

PSALMS.

4 He asked life of thee, and thou' gavest it him,
Even length of' days for ever and ever.
5 His glory is great in' thy sal-vation;
Honour and majesty' hast thou laid up-on him.
6 For thou hast made him most' blessed for ever;
Thou hast made him ex'ceeding glad with thy countenance.
7 For the king trusteth' in the LORD,
And through the mercy of the Most High' he shall not be moved.
8 Thine hand shall find out' all thine enemies:
Thy right hand shall' find out those that hate thee.
9 Thou shalt make them as a fiery oven in the time' of thine anger:
The Lord shall swallow them up in his wrath', and the fire shall de-vour them.
10 Their fruit shalt thou destroy' from the earth,
And their seed from a'mong the children of men.
11 For they intended' evil a-gainst thee:
They imagined a mischievous device, which they are not' a-ble to per-form:
12 Therefore shalt thou make them' turn their back,
When thou shalt make ready thine arrows upon thy strings a'gainst the face of them.
13 Be thou exalted, LORD, in' thine own strength:
So will we' sing and praise thy power.

PSALM XXII.

¶ To the chief Musician upon Aijeleth Shahar. A Psalm of David.

MY God, my God, why hast' thou for-saken me?
Why art thou so far from helping me, and from the' wörds of my roaring?
2 O my God, I cry in the daytime, but thou' hear-est not;
And in the night' season, and am not silent.

PSALMS.

3 But' thou art holy,
O thou that in'habitest the praises of Israel.
4 Our fathers' trusted in thee:
They trusted', and thou didst de-liver⌣them.
5 They cried unto thee, and' were de-livered:
They trusted in thee', and were not con-founded.
6 But I am a worm, and' nö man;
A reproach of men, and de'spis-ed of the people.
7 All they that see me' laugh⌣me to scorn:
They shoot out the' lip, they shake the⌣head, saying,
8 He trusted on the LORD that he' would de-liver⌣him:
Let him deliver him, seeing' he de-light-ed in⌣him.
9 But thou art he that took me' out of the⌣womb:
Thou didst make me hope when I was up'on my mo-ther's breasts.
10 I was cast upon thee' from the womb:
Thou art my God' from my mo-ther's belly.
11 Be not far from me, for' trouble is near;
For' there is none to help.
12 Many bulls have' compass-ed me:
Strong bulls of Bashan' have be-set me round.
13 They gaped upon me' with their mouths,
As a ravening' and a roar-ing lion.
14 I am poured out like water, and all my bones are' out of joint:
My heart is like wax; it is melted' in the⌣midst of my bowels.
15 My strength is dried up like a potsherd: and my tongue cleaveth' to my jaws;
And thou hast brought me' into the dust of death.
16 For dogs have compassed me: the assembly of the wicked' have in-closed⌣me:
They' pierced my hands and my⌣feet.
17 I may tell' all my bones:
They' look and stare up-on⌣me.

23

PSALMS.

18 They part my' garments a-mong‿them,
And cast' lots up-on my vesture.
19 But be not thou far from' me, O LORD:
O my' strength, haste thee to help‿me.
20 Deliver my soul' from the sword;
My darling' from the power of the‿dog.
21 Save me from the' li-on's mouth:
For thou hast heard me' from the horns of the‿ unicorns.
22 I will declare thy name un'to my brethren:
· In the midst of the congre'ga-tion will I praise‿ thee.
23 Ye that fear the LORD', präise him;
All ye the seed of Jacob, glorify him; and fear him, all' ye the seed of Israel.
24 For he hath not despised nor abhorred the afflic-tion' of the‿af-flicted,
Neither hath he hid his face from him; but when he cried' un-to him he heard.
25 My praise shall be of thee in the' great congre-ga-tion:
I will pay my vows be'före them that fear‿him.
26 The meek shall eat' and be satisfied:
They shall praise the LORD that seek him: your' heart shall live for ever.
27 All the ends of the world shall remember and turn un'to the LORD:
And all the kindreds of the nations shall' worship be-före thee.
28 For the kingdom' is the Lord's:
And he is the' governor a-mong the nations.
29 All they that be fat upon earth shall' eat and worship:
All they that go down to the dust shall bow before him: and none can' keep alive his own soul.
30 A' seed shall serve‿him;
It shall be accounted to the LORD' for a gen-er-ation.

24

31 They shall come, and shall declare his righteousness
   unto a people that' shall be born,
   That' hë hath done this.

PSALM XXIII.

¶ A Psalm of David.

THE Lord' is my shepherd;
   I' sḧäll not want.
2 He maketh me to lie down in' grëen pastures:
   He leadeth me be'side the still waters.
3 He re'storeth my soul:
   He leadeth me in the paths of' righteousness for
   his name's sake.
4 Yea, though I walk through the valley of the
   shadow of death, I will' fear no evil:
   For thou art with me; thy rod' and thy staff they
   comfort‿me.
5 Thou preparest a table before me in the presence' of
   mine enemies:
   Thou anointest my head with oil'; my cup runneth over.
6 Surely goodness and mercy shall follow me all the
   days' of my life:
   And I will dwell in the' house of the‿Lord for
   ever.

PSALM XXIV.

¶ A Psalm of David.

THE earth is the Lord's, and the' fulness there-of;
   The world, and' they that dwell there-in.
2 For he hath founded it up'on the seas,
   And established' it up-on the floods.
3 Who shall ascend into the' hill of the‿Lord?
   Or who shall stand' in his ho-ly place?

PSALMS.

4 He that hath clean hands', and‿a pure heart;
Who hath not lifted up his soul unto' vanity, nor sworn de-ceitfully.
5 He shall receive the' blessing from the‿Lord,
And righteousness from the' God of his sal-vation.
6 This is the generation of' them that seek‿him,
That' seek thy face, O Jacob. Selah.
7 Lift up your heads, O ye gates; and be ye lift up,
ye ever'-last-ing doors;
And the King of' glo-ry shall come in.
8 Who is this' King of glory?
The Lord strong and mighty, the' Lörd mighty in battle.
9 Lift up your heads, O ye gates; even lift them up,
ye ever'-last-ing doors:
And the King of' glo-ry shall come in.
10 Who is this' King of glory?
The Lord of hosts', he is the‿King of glory. Selah.

PSALM XXV.

¶ A Psalm of David.

UNTO' thee, O Lord,
Do' I lift up my soul.
2 O my God, I' trust in thee:
Let me not be ashamed; let not mine' ene-mies tri-umph over‿me.
3 Yea, let none that wait on thee' be a-shamed:
Let them be ashamed which trans'gress with-öut cause.
4 Show me thy' ways, O Lord;
T'ëach me thy paths.
5 Lead me in thy' truth, and teach‿me:
For thou art the God of my salvation; on thee do I' wäit all the day.
6 Remember, O Lord, thy tender mercies and' thy loving-kindnesses;
For they' have been ever of old.

PSALMS.

7 Remember not the sins of my youth, nor' my transgressions;
   According to thy mercy remember thou me for thy' good-ness' sake, O LORD.
8 Good and upright' is the LORD:
   Therefore will he teach' sin-ners in the way.
9 The meek will he' guide in judgment,
   And the meek' will he teach his way.
10 All the paths of the LORD are' mercy and truth
   Unto such as keep his' cove-nant and his testimonies.
11 For thy name's' sake, O LORD,
   Pardon mine i'niquity; for it is great.
12 What man is he that' feareth the LORD?
   Him shall he teach in the' way that he shall choose.
13 His soul shall' dwell at ease:
   And his seed' shall in-herit the earth.
14 The secret of the LORD is with' them that fear_him;
   And he will' shöw them his covenant.
15 Mine eyes are ever' toward the LORD;
   For he shall pluck my' feet out of the net.
16 Turn thee unto me, and have' mercy up-on_me;
   For I am' deso-late and af-flicted.
17 The troubles of my heart' are en-larged:
   O bring thou me' out of my dis-tresses.
18 Look upon mine affliction' and my pain;
   And for'gīve all my sins.
19 Consider mine enemies; for' they are many;
   And they' hate_me with cru-el hatred.
20 O keep my soul', and de-liver_me:
   Let me not be ashamed; for I' put my trust in thee.
21 Let integrity and up'rightness pre-serve_me;
   F'or I wait on thee.
22 Redeem' Israel, O God,
   O'ut of all his troubles.

PSALMS.

PSALM XXVI.
¶ A Psalm of David.

JUDGE me, O LORD; for I have walked in' mine in-tegrity:
I have trusted also in the LORD'; therefore I shall not slide.
2 Examine me, O' LORD, and prove me;
Try' my reins and my heart.
3 For thy lovingkindness is be'fore mine eyes;
And I have' walk-ed in thy truth.
4 I have not sat with' väin persons,
Neither will I' go in with dis-semblers.
5 I have hated the congregation of' e-vil doers;
And will' not sit with the wicked.
6 I will wash mine' hands in innocency:
So will I' compass thine altar, O LORD:
7 That I may publish with the' voice of thanksgiving,
And tell of' all thy won-drous works.
8 LORD, I have loved the habitation' of thy house,
And the place' where thine hon-our dwelleth.
9 Gather not my' soul with sinners,
Nor my' life with blood-y men:
10 In whose' hands is mischief,
And their right' hand is full of bribes.
11 But as for me, I will walk in' mine in-tegrity;
Redeem me, and be' merci-ful un-to me.
12 My foot standeth in an' e-ven place:
In the congregations' will I bless the LORD.

PSALM XXVII.
¶ A Psalm of David.

THE LORD is my light and my salvation; whom' shall I fear?
The LORD is the strength of my life; of whom' shall I be a-fraid?

PSALMS.

2 When the wicked, even mine enemies' and my foes,
Came upon me to eat up my flesh', thëy stumbled and fell.
3 Though an host should encamp against me, my heart' shall not fear:
Though war should rise against me, in' this will I be confident.
4 One thing have I desired of the Lord, that will' I seek after:
That I may dwell in the house of the Lord all the days of my life, to behold the beauty of the Lord, and to in'quīre in his temple.
5 For in the time of trouble he shall hide me in' his pa-vilion:
In the secret of his tabernacle shall he hide me; he shall' set‿me up-on a rock.
6 And now shall mine head be lifted up above mine enemies' round a-bout‿me:
Therefore will I offer in his tabernacle sacrifices of joy: I will sing, yea, I will sing' praises un-to the Lord.
7 Hear, O Lord, when I cry' with my voice:
Have mercy also up'ön me, and answer‿me.
8 When thou saidst, Seek' ye my face;
My heart said unto thee, Thy' face, Lord, wĭll I seek.
9 Hide not thy face far from me; put not thy servant a'way in anger;
Thou hast been my help; leave me not, neither forsake me, O' God of my sal-vation.
10 When my father and my' mother for-sake‿me,
Then the' Lord will take me up.
11 Teach me thy' way, O Lord,
And lead me in a plāin path, be'cäuse of mine enemies.
12 Deliver me not over unto the will' of mine enemies:
For false witnesses are risen up against me, and' such as breathe out cruelty.

PSALMS.

13 I had fainted, unless I had believed to see the
goodness' of the LORD
In the' länd of the living.
14 Wait on the LORD: be of good courage, and he
shall' strengthen thine heart:
Wait', I say, on the LORD.

PSALM XXVIII.

¶ A Psalm of David.

UNTO thee will I cry, O LORD, my rock; be not'
silent to me:
Lest, if thou be silent to me, I become like them
that' go down into the pit.
2 Hear the voice of my supplications, when I' cry
unto thee,
When I lift up my hands' toward thy ho-ly oracle.
3 Draw me not away with the wicked, and with the'
workers of iniquity;
Which speak peace to their neighbours, but'
mischief is in their hearts.
4 Give them according to their deeds, and according
to the wickedness of' their en-deavours:
Give them after the work of their hands; render to'
thëm their de-sert.
5 Because they regard not the works of the LORD,
nor the operation' of his hands,
He shall destroy them', and not build them up.
6 Blessed' be the LORD,
Because he hath heard the' voice of my sup-pli-
cations.
7 The LORD is my strength and my shield; my heart
trusted in him, and' I am helped:
Therefore my heart greatly rejoiceth, and with
my' söng will I praise him.
8 The LORD is' thëir strength,
And he is the saving' strength of his an-ointed.

PSALMS.

9 Save thy people, and' bless thine inheritance:
Feed them also, and' lift them up for ever.

PSALM XXIX.
¶ A Psalm of David.

GIVE unto the LORD', O ye mighty,
Give unto the' LÖRD glory and strength.
2 Give unto the LORD the glory due un'to his name;
Worship the' LORD in the‿beauty of holiness.
3 The voice of the LORD is up'on the waters:
The God of glory thundereth: the' LORD is upon many waters.
4 The voice of the' LORD is powerful;
The voice of the' LORD is full of majesty.
5 The voice of the LORD' breaketh the cedars;
Yea, the LORD' breaketh the cedars of Lebanon.
6 He maketh them also to' skip like‿a calf;
Lebanon and' Sirion like‿a yöung unicorn.
7 The voice' of the LORD
Di'videth the flames of fire:
8 The voice of the LORD' shaketh the wilderness;
The LORD' shaketh the wilderness of Kadesh.
9 The voice of the LORD maketh the hinds to calve, and dis'covereth the forests:
And in his temple doth' every one speak of‿his glory.
10 The LORD sitteth up'on the flood;
Yea, the' LORD sitteth King for ever.
11 The LORD will give strength' unto his people;
The LORD will' bless his people with peace.

PSALM XXX.
¶ A Psalm and Song at the dedication of the house of David.

I WILL ex'tol‿thee, O LORD;
For thou hast lifted me up, and hast not made my foes to re'jöice ov-er me.

PSALMS.

2 O' LORD my God,
I cried unto' thee, and thou hast healed‿me.
3 O LORD, thou hast brought up my' soul from the‿grave;
Thou hast kept me alive, that I should not' go down to the pit.
4 Sing unto the LORD, O ye' saints of his,
And give thanks at the re'mem-brance of his holiness.
5 For his anger endureth but a moment; in his' favour is life:
Weeping may endure for a night, but' joy cometh in the morning.
6 And in' my pros-perity
I said', I shall never be moved.
7 LORD, by thy favour thou hast made my mountain to' stånd strong:
Thou didst hide thy' face, and I was troubled.
8 I cried to' thee, O LORD;.
And unto the' LORD I made suppli-cation.
9 What profit is there in my blood, when I go' down to the‿pit?
Shall the dust praise thee? Shall' it de-clare thy truth?
10 Hear, O LORD, and have' mercy up-on‿me:
L'ORD, be thou my helper.
11 Thou hast turned for me my mourning' in-to dancing:
Thou hast put off my sackcloth, and' gird-ed me with gladness:
12 To the end that my glory may sing praise to thee, and' not be silent.
O LORD my God, I will give' thanks unto thee for ever.

PSALMS.

PSALM XXXI.

¶ To the Chief Musician, A Psalm of David.

IN thee, O Lord, do I′ put my trust;
　Let me never be ashamed: de′liver me in thy righteousness.
2 Bow down thine ear to me; de′liver me speedily:
　Be thou my strong rock, for an′ house of defence to save‿me.
3 For thou art my rock′ and my fortress;
　Therefore for thy name's sake′ lĕad me and gŭide‿me.
4 Pull me out of the net that they have′ laid privily for‿me:
　For′ thöu art my strength.
5 Into thine hand I com′mit my spirit:
　Thou hast redeemed me′, O Lord God of truth.
6 I have hated them that regard′ ly-ing vanities:
　But I′ trüst in the Lord.
7 I will be glad and rejoice′ in thy mercy:
　For thou hast considered my trouble; thou hast′ known my soul in adversities;
8 And hast not shut me up into the′ hand of the‿enemy:
　Thou hast set my′ fŏot in‿a large room.
9 Have mercy upon me, O Lord, for I′ am in trouble:
　Mine eye is consumed with grief, yea, my′ söul and my belly.
10 For my life is spent with grief, and my′ years with sighing:
　My strength faileth because of mine iniquity, and my′ bönes are con-sumed.
11 I was a reproach among all mine enemies, but especially a′mong my neighbours,
　And a fear to mine acquaintance: they that did′ see‿me with-out fled from‿me.
12 I am forgotten as a dead man′ out of mind:
　I am′ like a bro-ken vessel.

C

PSALMS.

13 For I have heard the slander of many: fear was on'
ev-ery side:
While they took counsel together against me, they
devised to' take a-way my life.
14 But I trusted in' thee, O LORD:
I' said, Thou art my God.
15 My times are' in thy hand:
Deliver me from the hand of mine enemies', and
from them that persecute me.
16 Make thy face to shine up'on thy servant:
Save me', for thy mer-cies' sake.
17 Let me not be ashamed, O LORD; for I have' called
up-on thee:
Let the wicked be ashamed, and let them be' si-lent
in the grave.
18 Let the lying lips be' put to silence:
Which speak grievous things proudly and con'-
temptuously a-gainst the righteous.
19 Oh how great is thy goodness, which thou hast laid
up for' them that fear thee;
Which thou hast wrought for them that trust in
thee be'fore the sons of men!
20 Thou shalt hide them in the secret of thy presence
from the' pride of man:
Thou shalt keep them secretly in a pavilion' from
the strife of tongues.
21 Blessed' be the LORD:
For he hath showed me his marvellous' kind-ness
in a strong city.
22 For I said in my haste, I am cut off from be'fore
thine eyes:
Nevertheless thou heardest the voice of my suppli-
cations' when I cried un-to thee.
23 O love the LORD, all' ye his saints:
For the LORD preserveth the faithful, and plenti-
fully re'wardeth the proud doer.
24 Be of good courage, and he shall' strengthen your heart,
All ye that' hope in the LORD.

PSALMS.

PSALM XXXII.

¶ A Psalm of David, Maschil.

BLESSED is he whose transgression' is for-given,
Wh'öse sin is covered.
2 Blessed is the man unto whom the LORD imputeth'
not i-niquity,
And in whose' spirit there is no guile.
3 When' I kept silence,
My bones waxed old through my' roar-ing all
the day long:
4 For day and night thy hand was' heavy up-on me:
My moisture is turned' into the drought of summer. Selah.
5 I acknowledged my sin unto thee, and mine iniquity have' I not hid.
I said, I will confess my transgressions unto the
LORD; and thou forgavest the i'niqui-ty of my
sin. Selah.
6 For this shall every one that is godly pray unto
thee in a time when thou' mayest be found:
Surely in the floods of great waters they shall' not
come nigh un-to him.
7 Thou art my hiding-place; thou shalt pro'serve me
from trouble;
Thou shalt compass me a'bout with songs of deliverance. Selah.
8 I will instruct thee and teach thee in the way
which' thou shalt go:
I will' guide thee with mine eye.
9 Be ye not as the horse, or as the mule, which have'
no under-standing:
Whose mouth must be held in with bit and bridle,
lest' they come near un-to thee.
10 Many sorrows shall' be to the wicked:
But he that trusteth in the LORD, mercy shall'
com-pass him a-bout.

PSALMS.

11 Be glad in the LORD, and re'joice, ye righteous;
And shout for joy, all ye' that are upright in heart.

PSALM XXXIII.

REJOICE in the LORD', O ye righteous:
For praise is' come-ly for the upright.
2 Praise the' LORD with harp:
Sing unto him with the psaltery and an' instru-ment of ten strings.
3 Sing unto him a' nëw song;
Play' skilful-ly with a loud noise.
4 For the word of the' LORD is right;
And all his' works are done in truth.
5 He loveth' righteousness and judgment:
The earth is full of the' good-ness of the LORD.
6 By the word of the LORD were the' hea-vens made;
And all the host of them by the' brëath of his mouth.
7 He gathereth the waters of the sea together' as an heap:
He layeth' up the depth in storehouses.
8 Let all the earth' fear the LORD:
Let all the inhabitants of the world' stand in awe of him:
9 For he spake, and' it was done;
He commanded', and it stöod fast.
10 The LORD bringeth the counsel of the' heathen to nought:
He maketh the devices of the' people of none ef-fect.
11 The counsel of the LORD' standeth for ever,
The thoughts of his' heart to all gene-rations.
12 Blessed is the nation whose' God is the LORD;
And the people whom he hath chosen' for his own in-heritance.
13 The LORD' looketh from heaven;
He beholdeth' all the sons of men.

PSALMS.

14 From the place of his' ha-bi-tation
   He looketh upon all the in'habi-tants of the earth.
15 He fashioneth their' hearts a-like;
   He con'sider-eth all their works.
16 There is no king saved by the multitude' of an host;
   A mighty man is not de'liver-ed by much strength.
17 An horse is a vain' thing for safety:
   Neither shall he deliver' any by his great strength.
18 Behold, the eye of the LORD is upon' them that fear‿him,
   Upon' them that hope in‿his mercy;
19 To deliver their' soul from death,
   And to' keep them alive in famine.
20 Our soul' waiteth for the‿LORD:
   He is our' hëlp and our shield.
21 For our heart shall re'joice in him;
   Because we have trusted' in his ho-ly name.
22 Let thy mercy, O' LORD, be upon‿us,
   According' as we hope in thee.

PSALM XXXIV.

¶ A Psalm of David, when he changed his behaviour before Abimelech; who drove him away, and he departed.

I WILL bless the' LORD at all‿times:
   His praise shall con'tinually be in my mouth.
2 My soul shall make her' boast in the‿LORD:
   The humble shall' hear thereof, and be glad.
3 O magnify the' LORD with me,
   And let us ex'alt his name to-gethér.
4 I sought the LORD', and he heard‿me,
   And delivered' me from all my fears.
5 They looked unto him', and were lightened:
   And their' faces were not a-shamed.
6 This poor man cried, and the' LÖRD heard‿him,
   And saved him' out of all his troubles.

PSALMS.

7 The angel' of the LORD
Encampeth round about them that' fear him, and
de-livereth‿them.
8 O taste and see that the' LORD is good:
Blessed is the' man that trusteth in him.
9 O fear the LORD', ye his saints:
For there is no' want to them that fear‿him.
10 The young lions do lack and' suf-fer hunger:
But they that seek the LORD shall not' wänt any‿
good thing.
11 Come, ye children', hearken unto me:
I will' teach you the‿fear of the‿LORD.
12 What man is he that de'sir-eth life,
And loveth many days, that' he may sëe good?
13 Keep thy' tongue from evil,
And thy' lips from speak-ing guile.
14 Depart from evil', and do good;
Seek' pëace, and pur-sue‿it.
15 The eyes of the LORD are up'on the righteous,
And his ears are' open un-to their cry.
16 The face of the LORD is against' them that‿do evil,
To cut off the remembrance' of them from the earth.
17 The righteous cry, and the' LÖRD heareth,
And delivereth them' out of all their troubles.
18 The LORD is nigh unto them that are of a' bro-ken
heart;
And saveth such as' be of‿a con-trite spirit.
19 Many are the afflictions' of the righteous:
But the LORD delivereth him' oüt of them all.
20 He keepeth' all his bones:
Not' one of them is broken.
21 Evil shall' slay the wicked:
And they that hate the' right-eous shall be desolate.
22 The LORD redeemeth the' soul of‿his servants:
And none of them that' trust in him shall‿be
desolate.

PSALM XXXV.

¶ A Psalm of David.

PLEAD my cause, O Lord, with them that' strive with me;
Fight against' them that fight against me.
2 Take hold of' shield and buckler,
And' stand up for mine help.
3 Draw out also the spear, and stop the way against' them that persecute‿me:
Say unto my soul', I am thy sal-vation.
4 Let them be confounded and put to shame that seek' after my soul:
Let them be turned back and brought to con'fusion that devise my hurt.
5 Let them be as chaff be'fore the wind:
And let the' angel of the‿Lörd chase‿them.
6 Let their way be' dark and slippery:
And let the' an-gel of the‿Lord persecute‿them.
7 For without cause have they hid for me their' net in a‿pit,
Which without cause they have' dig-ged for my soul.
8 Let destruction come upon him' at una-wares;
And let his net that he hath hid catch himself:
into that very de'struc-tion let him fall.
9 And my soul shall be' joyful in the‿Lord:
It shall re'joice in his sal-vation.
10 All my bones shall say, Lord, who is' like unto thee,
Which deliverest the poor from him that is too strong for him, yea, the poor and the' needy from him that spoileth‿him?
11 False witnesses did' rïse up;
They laid to my charge' thïngs that I knew‿not.
12 They rewarded me' evil for good,
To the' spoil-ing of my soul.

PSALMS.

13 But as for me, when they were sick, my' clothing was sackcloth:
I humbled my soul with fasting; and my prayer returned' into mine öwn bosom.
14 I behaved myself as though he had been my' friend or brother:
I bowed down heavily, as one that' mourn-eth for his mother.
15 But in mine adversity they rejoiced, and gathered them'selves to-gether:
Yea, the abjects gathered themselves together against me, and I knew it not; they did' tear⁀me, and ceas-ed not:
16 With hypocritical' mockers in feasts,
They gnashed up'on me with their teeth.
17 LORD, how long wilt' thou look on?
Rescue my soul from their destructions, my' dar-ling from the lions.
18 I will give thee thanks in the' great congre-ga-tion:
I will' praise thee⁀a-mong much people.
19 Let not them that are mine enemies wrongfully re'joice over me;
Neither let them wink with the eye that' hate⁀me with-out a cause.
20 For they' speak not peace;
But they devise deceitful matters against them that are' qui-et in the land.
21 Yea, they opened their mouth wide a'gainst⁀me, and said,
Aha, a'ha! our eye hath seen⁀it.
22 This thou hast' seen, O LORD;
Keep not silence: O' LORD, be not far from⁀me.
23 Stir up thyself, and a'wake to⁀my judgment,
Even unto my cause', my God and my LORD.
24 Judge me, O LORD my God, according to' thÿ righteousness;
And let them not re'jöice o-ver me.

PSALMS.

25 Let them not say in their hearts, Ah', so would‿we have‿it:
 Let them not say', We have swallowed him up.
26 Let them be ashamed and brought to confusion together that rejoice' at mine hurt:
 Let them be clothed with shame and dishonour that' magnify them-selves a-gainst‿me.
27 Let them shout for joy, and be glad, that favour my' right-eous cause:
 Yea, let them say continually, Let the LORD be magnified, which hath pleasure in the pros'peri-ty of his servant.
28 And my tongue shall' speak of‿thy righteousness,
 And of thy' präise, all the‿day long.

PSALM XXXVI.

¶ To the chief Musician, A Psalm of David the servant of the LORD.

THE transgression of the wicked saith with'in my heart,
 That there is no fear of' God be-fore his eyes.
2 For he flattereth himself in' his own eyes,
 Until his iniquity be' found to be hateful.
3 The words of his mouth are iniquity' and de-ceit:
 He hath left off to be' wise, and to do good.
4 He deviseth mischief up'on his bed;
 · He setteth himself in a way that is not good'; he ab-horreth not evil.
5 Thy mercy, O LORD, is' in the heavens,
 And thy faithfulness' reacheth un-to the clouds.
6 Thy righteousness is like the great mountains; thy judgments' are a‿great deep:
 O LORD, thou pre'serv-est man and beast.
7 How excellent is thy loving'kindness, O God!
 Therefore the children of men put their trust under the' sha-dow of thy wings.

PSALMS.

8 They shall be abundantly satisfied with the fatness'
 of thy house;
 And thou shalt make them drink of the' riv-er of
 thy pleasures.
9 For with thee is the' fountain of life:
 In thy' light shall we see light.
10 O continue thy lovingkindness unto' them that
 know‿thee;
 And thy' righteousness to the‿upright in heart.
11 Let not the foot of pride' come a-gainst‿me,
 And let not the' hand of the‿wicked re-move‿me.
12 There are the workers of i'niqui-ty fallen:
 They are cast down, and shall' not be able to rise.

PSALM XXXVII.
¶ A Psalm of David.

FRET not thyself because of' e-vil-doers,
 Neither be thou envious against the' work-ers of
 i-niquity:
2 For they shall soon be cut' down like the‿grass,
 And' wither as the‿green herb.
3 Trust in the LORD', and do good;
 So shalt thou dwell in the land, and' verily thou
 shalt be fed.
4 Delight thyself also' in the LORD;
 And he shall give thee the de'sires of thine heart.
5 Commit thy way un'to the LORD;
 Trust also in him, and' he shall bring‿it to pass:
6 And he shall bring forth thy righteousness' as the
 light,
 And thy' judg-ment as the noonday.
7 Rest in the LORD, and wait' patient-ly for‿him:
 Fret not thyself because of him who prospereth in
 his way, because of the man who bringeth'
 wicked de-vices to pass.
8 Cease from anger, and for'sake wrath:
 Fret not thyself in' any wise to do evil.

PSALMS.

9 For evil-doers' shall be‿cut off:
But those that wait upon the Lord', they shall inherit the earth.
10 For yet a little while, and the wicked' shall not be:
Yea, thou shalt diligently consider his place', and it shall not be.
11 But the meek shall in'herit the earth,
And shall delight themselves' in the‿a-bundance of peace.
12 The wicked plotteth a'gainst the just,
And gnasheth up'on him with his teeth.
13 The Lord shall' laugh at him:
For he' seeth that his‿day is coming.
14 The wicked have drawn out the sword, and have' bent their bow,
To cast down the poor and needy, and to slay such as be of' up-right con-ver-sation.
15 Their sword shall enter into' their own heart,
And their' bōws shall be broken.
16 A little that a' righteous man hath
Is better than the' riches of ma-ny wicked.
17 For the arms of the wicked' shall be broken:
But the' Lord up-holdeth the righteous.
18 The Lord knoweth the' days of the‿upright:
And their in'heritance shall be for ever.
19 They shall not be ashamed in the' e-vil time:
And in the days of' famine they shall be satisfied.
20 But the wicked shall perish, and the enemies of the Lord shall be as the' fat of lambs:
They shall consume; into smoke shall' they con-sume a-way.
21 The wicked borroweth, and' payeth not again;
But the' righteous showeth mercy, and giveth.
22 For such as be blessed of him shall in'herit the earth;
And they that be cursed of' him shall be cut off.
23 The steps of a good man are' ordered by the‿Lord;
And he de'light-eth in his way.

PSALMS.

24 Though he fall, he shall not be' utterly cast down:
For the LORD up'holdeth him with his hand.
25 I have been young, and' now am old;
Yet have I not seen the righteous forsaken', nor his seed begging bread.
26 He is ever' merciful, and lendeth;
And' his seed is blessed.
27 Depart from evil', and do good;
And' dwell for e-ver-more.
28 For the LORD loveth judgment, and forsaketh' not his saints;
They are preserved for ever: but the seed of the' wicked shall be cut off.
29 The righteous shall in'herit the land,
And' dwell there-in for ever.
30 The mouth of the righteous' speak-eth wisdom,
And his' töngue talketh of judgment.
31 The law of his God is' in his heart;
N'one of his steps shall slide.
32 The wicked' watcheth the righteous,
And' sëek-eth to slay him.
33 The LORD will not leave him' in his hand,
Nor con'demn him when he is judged.
34 Wait on the LORD, and keep his way, and he shall exalt thee to in'herit the land:
When the wicked are' cut off, thou shalt see it.
35 I have seen the wicked in' grëat power,
And spreading him'self like a green bay tree.
36 Yet he passed away, and', lo, he was not:
Yea, I sought him, but' he could not be found.
37 Mark the perfect man, and be'hold the upright:
For the' end of that man is peace.
38 But the transgressors shall be de'stroyed together:
The end of the' wicked shall be cut off.
39 But the salvation of the righteous' is of the LORD:
He is their' strength in the time of trouble.

40 And the LORD shall help them', and de-liver‿them:
He shall deliver them from the wicked, and save
them, be'cause they trust in him.

PSALM XXXVIII.

¶ A Psalm of David, to bring to remembrance.

O LORD, rebuke me not' in thy wrath;
Neither chasten me' in thy hot dis-pleasure.
2 For thine arrows' stick fast in‿me,
And' thy hand presseth me sore.
3 There is no soundness in my flesh', because of‿thine anger;
Neither is there any rest in my bones, be'cäuse of my sin.
4 For mine iniquities are gone' over mine head:
As an heavy burden' they are too heavy for‿me.
5 My wounds stink, and' are cor-rupt,
Be'cäuse of my foolishness.
6 I am troubled; I am' bowed down greatly;
I go' mourn-ing all the‿day long.
7 For my loins are filled with a' loathsome dis-ease:
And there is no' sound-ness in my flesh.
8 I am feeble and' sore broken:
I have roared by reason of the dis'quiet-ness of my heart.
9 LORD, all my desire' is be-fore‿thee;
And my' groaning is not hid from‿thee.
10 My heart panteth, my' strëngth faileth‿me:
As for the light of mine eyes', it also is gone from‿me.
11 My lovers and my friends stand aloof' from my sore;
And my' kins-men stand afar off.
12 They also that seek after my life lay' snäres for‿me;
And they that seek my hurt speak mischievous things, and imagine de'cëits all the‿day long.

45

13 But I, as a' deaf man, heard not;
   And I was as a dumb man that' open-eth not his mouth.
14 Thus I was as a' man that heareth not,
   And in whose' mouth are no re-proofs.
15 For in thee, O LORD', do I hope:
   Thou wilt' hear, O LORD my God.
16 For I said, Hear me; lest otherwise they should re'jöice over me:
   When my foot slippeth, they' magnify them-selves a-gainst me.
17 For I am' ready to halt,
   And my sorrow' is con-tinually be-fore me.
18 For I will de'clare mine iniquity;
   I will be' sor-ry for my sin.
19 But mine enemies are lively, and' they are strong:
   And they that' hate me wrongfully are multiplied.
20 They also that render evil for good' are mine adversaries;
   Because I follow the' thing that göod is.
21 Forsake me' not, O LORD:
   O my' God, be not far from me.
22 Make' haste to help me,
   O' LÖRD, my sal-vation.

PSALM XXXIX.

¶ To the chief Musician, even to Jeduthun, A Psalm of David.

I SAID, I will take heed to my ways, that I sin not' with my tongue;
   I will keep my mouth with a bridle, while the' wick-ed is be-fore me.
2 I was' dumb with silence,
   I held my peace, even from good'; and my sorrow was stirred.
3 My heart was' hot with-in me;
   While I was musing the fire burned: then' spake I with my tongue,

PSALMS.

4 LORD, make me to know mine end, and the measure
of my days', what it is;
That I may' know how frail I am.
5 Behold, thou hast made my days as an handbreadth;
and mine age is as' nothing be-fore‿thee:
Verily, every man at his best state is' al-to-ge-ther
vanity. Selah.
6 Surely every man walketh in a vain show; surely
they are' disquieted in vain:
He heapeth up riches, and' knoweth not who shall
gather‿them.
7 And now, LORD, what' wait I for?
My' höpe is in thee.
8 Deliver me from' all my transgressions;
Make me not the re'pröach of the foolish.
9 I was dumb, I opened' not my mouth;
Be'cäuse thöu didst‿it.
10 Remove thy' stroke away from‿me;
I am consumed by the' blöw of thine hand.
11 When thou with rebukes dost correct' man for
iniquity,
Thou makest his beauty to consume away like a
moth: surely' ev-ery man is vanity. Selah.
12 Hear my prayer, O LORD, and give ear unto my
cry; hold not thy' peace at my‿tears:
For I am a stranger with thee, and a sojourner, as'
all my fa-thers were.
13 O spare me, that I may re'cover my strength,
Before I go' hence, and be no more.

PSALM XL.

¶ To the chief Musician, A Psalm of David.

I WAITED patiently' for the LORD:
And he inclined unto' me, and heard my cry.
2 He brought me up also out of an horrible pit, out
of the' mi-ry clay,
And set my feet upon a rock', and es-tablished my
goings.

PSALMS.

3 And he hath put a new song in my mouth, even praise un'to our God:
Many shall see it, and fear, and shall' trüst in the LORD.
4 Blessed is that man that maketh the' LORD his trust;
And respecteth not the proud, nor such as' turn a-side to lies.
5 Many, O LORD my God, are thy wonderful works which thou hast done, and thy thoughts which' are to usward:
They cannot be reckoned up in order unto thee: if I would declare and speak of them, they are' more than can be numbered.
6 Sacrifice and offering thou didst not desire; mine ears' hast thou opened:
Burnt-offering and sin-offering' hast thou not required.
7 Then said I', Lo, I come:
In the volume of the' book it is written of me,
8 I delight to do thy will', O my God:
Yea, thy' law is within my heart.
9 I have preached righteousness in the' great congregation:
Lo, I have not refrained my' lips, O˙ LORD, thou knowest.
10 I have not hid thy righteousness within my heart:
I have declared thy faithfulness and' thy salvation:
I have not concealed thy loving-kindness and thy truth from the' grëat con-gre-gation.
11 Withhold not thou thy tender mercies from' me, O LORD:
Let thy loving-kindness and thy' truth con-tinually pre-serve me.
12 For innumerable evils have' compassed me about:
Mine iniquities have taken hold upon me, so that I am not able to look up; they are more than the hairs of mine head: therefore my' hëart fail-eth me.

PSALMS.

13 Be pleased, O LORD, to de′liv-er me:
O′ LORD, make haste to help me.
14 Let them be ashamed and confounded together that seek after my′ soul to destroy it;
Let them be driven backward and put to′ shame that wish me evil.
15 Let them be desolate for a reward′ of their shame, That say unto′ me, A-ha, a-ha!
16 Let all those that seek thee rejoice and be′ glad in thee:
Let such as love thy salvation say con′tinually, The LORD be magnified.
17 But I am poor and needy; yet the LORD′ thinketh up-on me:
Thou art my help and my deliverer; make no′ tarry-ing, O my God.

PSALM XLI.

¶ To the chief Musician, A Psalm of David.

BLESSED is he that con′sidereth the poor:
The LORD will de′liver him in time of trouble.
2 The LORD will preserve him, and keep him alive; and he shall be blessed up′on the earth:
And thou wilt not deliver him un′to the will of his enemies.
3 The LORD will strengthen him upon the′ bed of languishing:
Thou wilt make all his′ bed in his sickness.
4 I said, LORD, be merciful′ un-to me:
Heal my soul; for′ I have sinned a-gainst thee.
5 Mine enemies speak′ evil of me;
When shall he′ die, and his name perish?
6 And if he come to see me, he′ speak-eth vanity:
His heart gathereth iniquity to itself; when he goeth a-broad, he telleth it.

PSALMS.

7 All that hate me whisper to'gether a-gainst‿me:
Against me do' they de-vise my hurt.
8 An evil disease, say they, cleaveth' fast un-to‿him:
And now that he lieth, he' shall rise up no more.
9 Yea, mine own familiar friend, in' whom I trusted,
Which did eat of my bread, hath lifted' up his heel a-gainst‿me.
10 But thou, O LORD, be merciful' un-to me,
And raise me up', that I may re-quite‿them.
11 By this I know that thou' favour-est me,
Because mine enemy' doth not tri-umph over‿me.
12 And as for me, thou upholdest me in' mine in-tegrity,
And settest me be'fore thy face for ever.
13 Blessed be the LORD God of Israel from everlast-ing, and to' e-ver-lasting.
A'mën, and a-men.

PSALM XLII.

¶ To the chief Musician, Maschil, for the sons of Korah.

AS the hart panteth after the' wa-ter brooks,
So panteth my' soul after thee, O God.
2 My soul thirsteth for God, for the' liv-ing God:
When shall I come and ap'pear be-fŏre God?
3 My tears have been my meat' day and night,
While they continually say unto me', Whëre is thy God?
4 When I remember these things, I pour out' my soul in‿me:
For I had gone with the multitude, I went with them to the house of God, with the voice of joy and praise, with a' multi-tude that kept holyday.
5 Why art thou cast down, O my soul? and why art thou dis'quieted in me?
Hope thou in God: for I shall yet praise him for the' hëlp of his countenance.

PSALMS.

6 O my God, my soul is cast' down with-in‿me:
  Therefore will I remember thee from the land of Jordan, and of the' Hermon-ites, from the‿hill Mizar.
7 Deep calleth unto deep at the' noise of‿thy water-spouts:
  All thy waves and thy' bil-lows are gone over‿me.
8 Yet the LORD will command his lovingkindness' in the daytime,
  And in the night his song shall be with me, and my prayer un'to the‿God of my life.
9 I will say unto God my rock, Why hast' thou for-gotten‿me?
  Why go I mourning because of the op'pres-sion of the enemy?
10 As with a sword in my bones, mine' enemies re-proach‿me;
  While they say daily unto me,' Whëre is thy God?
11 Why art thou cast down, O my soul? And why art thou dis'quieted with-in‿me?
  Hope thou in God; for I shall yet praise him, who is the health of my' counte-nance, and my God.

PSALM XLIII.

JUDGE me, O God, and plead my cause against an un'god-ly nation:
  O deliver me from the de'ceitful and un-just man.
2 For thou art the God of my strength: why dost thou' cast me off?
  Why go I mourning because of the op'pres-sion of the enemy?
3 O send out thy light and thy truth': let them lead‿me;
  Let them bring me unto thy holy' hill, and to thy tabernacles.

PSALMS.

4 Then will I go unto the altar of God, unto God
my ex′ceed-ing joy:
Yea, upon the harp will I′ praise‿thee, O God, my
God.
5 Why art thou cast down, O my soul? and why art
thou dis′quieted with-in‿me?
Hope in God: for I shall yet praise him, who is
the health of my′ counte-nance, and my God.

PSALM XLIV.

¶ To the chief Musician for the sons of Korah, Maschil.

WE have heard with our ears, O God, our′ fathers
have told‿us,
What work thou didst in their days′, in the times
of old.
2 How thou didst drive out the heathen with thy
hand, and′ plant-edst them;
How thou didst afflict the′ people, and cast them
out.
3 For they got not the land in possession by
their own sword, neither did their′ own arm
save‿them:
But thy right hand, and thine arm, and the light
of thy countenance, because thou′ hadst a
favour un-to‿them.
4 Thou art my′ King, O God:
Com′mand de-liverances for Jacob.
5 Through thee will we push′ down our enemies:
Through thy name will we tread them under that′
rise up a-gainst‿us.
6 For I will not trust′ in my bow,
Neither′ shall my sword save‿me.
7 But thou hast saved us′ from our enemies,
And hast put′ them to shame that hated‿us.
8 In God we boast′ all the‿day long,
And′ praise thy name for ever. Selah.

PSALMS.

9 But thou hast cast off, and' put‿us to shame;
And goest not' förth with our armies.
10 Thou makest us to turn' back from the‿enemy:
And they which' hate‿us spoil for them-selves.
11 Thou hast given us like sheep ap'pointed for meat;
And hast' scattered us among the heathen.
12 Thou sellest thy' people for nought,
And dost not increase thy' wĕalth by their price.
13 Thou makest us a re'proach to‿our neighbours,
A scorn and a derision to' them that‿are round
a-bout‿us.
14 Thou makest us a byword a'mong the heathen,
A shaking of the' head a-mong the people.
15 My confusion is con'tinually be-fore‿me,
And the shame' of my face hath covered‿me,
16 For the voice of him that reproacheth' and blas-
phemeth;
By reason of the' ene-my and a-venger.
17 All this is' come up-on‿us;
Yet have we not forgotten thee, neither have we
dealt' false-ly in thy covenant.
18 Our heart is not' turn-ed back,
Neither have our steps de'clin-ed from thy way;
19 Though thou hast sore broken us in the' place of
dragons,
And covered us' with the shadow of death.
20 If we have forgotten the' name of‿our God,
Or stretched out our' hands to‿a strănge god;
21 Shall not God' search this out?
For he knoweth the' se-crets of the heart.
22 Yea, for thy sake are we killed' all the‿day long;
We are counted as' shëep for the slaughter.
23 Awake, why sleepest' thou, O LORD?
Arise', cast‿us not off for ever.
24 Wherefore hidest' thou thy face,
And forgettest our af'fliction and our op-pression?
25 For our soul is bowed' down to the‿dust:
Our belly' cleaveth un-to the earth.

53

PSALMS.

26 Arise' for our help,
And redeem us' for thy mer-cies' sake.

PSALM XLV.

To the chief Musician upon Shoshannim, for the sons of Korah, Maschil, A song of loves.

MY heart is inditing a' göod matter:
I speak of the things which I have made touching the˙king: my tongue is the' pen of˷a rea-dy writer.
2 Thou art fairer than the' children of men:
Grace is poured into thy lips: therefore God hath' bless-ed thee for ever.
3 Gird thy sword upon thy thigh', O most mighty,
With thy' glo-ry and thy majesty.
4 And in thy majesty ride prosperously because of truth and' meekness and righteousness;
And thy right hand shall' teach thee terri-ble things.
5 Thine arrows are sharp in the heart' of the˷king's enemies;
Whereby the' people fall un-der thee.
6 Thy throne, O God, is for' ever and ever:
The sceptre of thy' king-dom is a˷right sceptre.
7 Thou lovest righteousness, and' ha-test wickedness:
Therefore God, thy God, hath anointed thee with the oil of' gladness a-bove thy fellows.
8 All thy garments smell of myrrh, and' aloes, and cassia,
Out of the ivory palaces, whereby' they have made thee glad.
9 Kings' daughters were among thy' honour-able women:
Upon thy right hand did stand the' queen in gold of Ophir.
10 Hearken, O daughter, and consider, and in'cline thine ear;
Forget also thine own people', and thy fa-ther's house;

PSALMS.

11 So shall the king greatly de′sire thy beauty:
For he is thy′ LORD; and worship thou him.
12 And the daughter of Tyre shall be′ there with
a gift;
Even the rich among the people′ shall en-treat thy
favour.
13 The king's daughter is all′ glorious with-in:
Her′ clothing is of wrought gold.
14 She shall be brought unto the king in′ raiment of
needlework:
The virgins her companions that follow her′ shall
be brought unto thee.
15 With gladness and rejoicing shall′ they be brought:
They shall′ enter in-to the king's palace.
16 Instead of thy fathers shall′ be thy children,
Whom thou mayest make′ princes in all the earth.
17 I will make thy name to be remembered in′ all
gene-rations:
Therefore shall the people′ praise thee for ever and
ever.

PSALM XLVI.

¶ To the chief Musician for the sons of Korah,
A Song upon Alamoth.

GOD is our′ refuge and strength,
A very′ pre-sent help in trouble.
2 Therefore will not we fear, though the′ earth be
removed,
And though the mountains be carried′ into the
midst of the sea;
3 Though the waters thereof′ roar and be troubled,
Though the mountains′ shake with the swelling
there-of. Selah.
4 There is a river, the streams whereof shall make
glad the′ city of God,
The holy place of the′ tabernacles of the Möst
High.

PSALMS.

5 God is in the midst of her; she shall' not be moved:
God shall' help‿her, and that right early.
6 The heathen raged, the' kingdoms were moved:
He uttered his' voice, the ëarth melted.
7 The LORD of' hosts is with‿us;
The God of' Ja-cob is our refuge. Selah.
8 Come, behold the' works of the‿LORD,
What desolations' he hath made in the‿earth.
9 He maketh wars to cease unto the' end of the‿earth;
He breaketh the bow, and cutteth the spear in sunder; he burneth the' cha-riot in the fire.
10 Be still, and know that' I am God:
I will be exalted among the heathen, I will be ex'alt-ed in the earth.
11 The LORD of' hosts is with‿us;
The God of' Ja-cob is our refuge. Selah.

PSALM XLVII.

¶ To the chief Musician, A Psalm for the sons of Korah.

O CLAP your hands', all ye people;
Shout unto' God with the‿voice of triumph.
2 For the LORD most' high is terrible;
He is a great' King over all the earth.
3 He shall subdue the' peo-ple under‿us,
And the' na-tions under our feet.
4 He shall choose our in'herit-ance for‿us,
The excellency of' Ja-cob whom he loved. Selah.
5 God is gone' up with a‿shout,
The' LORD with the‿sound of a‿trumpet.
6 Sing praises to' God, sing praises:
Sing praises' unto our King, sing praises.
7 For God is the King of' all the earth:
Sing ye' praises with un-der-stand-ing.
8 God reigneth' over the heathen:
God sitteth upon the' thröne of his holiness.

PSALMS.

9 The princes of the people are gathered together,
even the people of the' God of Abraham:
For the shields of the earth belong unto God': he
is greatly ex-alted.

PSALM XLVIII.

¶ A Song and Psalm for the sons of Korah.

G REAT is the LORD, and' greatly to‿be praised
In the city of our God, in the' moun-tain of his
holiness.
2 Beautiful for situation, the joy of the whole earth',
is mount Zion,
On the sides of the north, the' city of the‿grëat
King.
3 God' is known
In her' pala-ces for a refuge.
4 For, lo, the' kings were assembled,
They' pass-ed by to-gether.
5 They saw it, and' so they marvelled;
They were' troubled, and hasted a-way.
6 Fear took hold' upon them there,
And pain', as of a‿woman in travail.
7 Thou breakest the' ships of Tarshish
W'ith an ëast wind.
8 As we have heard, so have we seen in the city of
the LORD of hosts, in the city' of our God:
God will es'tab-lish it for ever. Selah.
9 We have thought of thy loving' kindness, O God,
In the' midst of thy temple.
10 According to thy name, O God, so is thy praise
unto the' ends of the‿earth:
Thy' right‿hand is full of righteousness.
11 Let mount' Zion re-joice,
Let the daughters of Judah be glad, be'cäuse of thy
judgments.
12 Walk about Zion, and go' round a-bout‿her:
T'ell the towers there-of.

PSALMS.

13 Mark ye well her bulwarks, con'sider her palaces:
That ye may tell it' to the‿gene-ra-tion following.
14 For this God is our God for' ever and ever:
He will be our guide' e-ven un-to death.

PSALM XLIX.

¶ To the chief Musician, A Psalm for the sons of Korah.

HEAR this', all ye people;
Give ear, all ye in'habit-ants of the world:
2 Both' low and high,
R'ich, and poor to-gether.
3 My mouth shall' speak of wisdom;
And the meditation of my heart shall' be of und-er-standing.
4 I will incline mine' ear to a‿parable:
I will open my dark' saying up-on the harp.
5 Wherefore should I fear in the' days of evil,
When the iniquity of my heels shall' com-pass me a-bout?
6 They that trust' in their wealth,
And boast themselves in the' multi-tude of their riches;
7 None of them can by any means re'deem his brother,
Nor give to' God a ran-som for‿him:
8 (For the redemption of their' soul is precious,
And' it ceaseth for ever:)
9 That he should still' live for ever,
A'nd not see cor-ruption.
10 For he seeth that' wise men die,
Likewise the fool and the brutish person perish,
and' leave their wealth to others.
11 Their inward thought is, that their houses shall continue for ever, and their dwelling places to' all gene-rations;
They call their lands' after their öwn names.

PSALMS.

12 Nevertheless man being in honour' abid-eth not:
   He is' like the beasts that perish.
13 This their way' is their folly:
   Yet their pos'terity ap-prove their sayings. Selah.
14 Like sheep they are laid in the grave; death' shall feed on_them;
   And the upright shall have dominion over them in the morning; and their beauty shall consume in the' gräve from their dwelling.
15 But God will redeem my soul from the' power of the_grave:
   For' hë shall re-ceive_me. Selah.
16 Be not thou afraid when one' is made rich,
   When the glory of his' höuse is in-creased;
17 For when he dieth he shall carry' nothing a-way:
   His glory shall' not de-scënd after_him.
18 Though, while he lived, he' blessed his soul:
   And men will praise thee when thou' doest well to thy-self.
19 He shall go to the generation' of his fathers;
   They' shäll never see light.
20 Man that is in honour, and under'stand-eth not,
   Is' like the beasts that perish.

PSALM L.

¶ A Psalm of Asaph.

THE mighty God, even the' LORD, hath spoken,
   And called the earth from the rising of the sun unto the' go-ing down there-of.
2 O'ut of Zion,
   The perfection of' beau-ty, God hath shined.
3 Our God shall come, and shall' not keep si-lence:
   A fire shall devour before him, and it shall be very tem'pestu-ous round a-bout_him.

PSALMS.

4 He shall call to the' heavens from above,
And to the earth, that' he may judge his people.
5 Gather my saints together' un-to me;
Those that have made a' covenant with me by sacrifice.
6 And the heavens shall de'clare his righteousness:
For' God is judge him-self. Selah.
7 Hear, O my people, and I will speak; O Israel, and I will' testify a-gainst‿thee:
I' am God, even thy God.
8 I will not reprove thee for thy sacrifices or' thy burnt offerings,
To have' been con-tinually be-fore‿me.
9 I will take no bullock' out‿of thy house,
Nor' he‿goats out of thy folds.
10 For every beast of the' forest is mine,
And the cattle up'on a thou-sand hills.
11 I know all the' fowls of the‿mountains:
And the wild beasts' of the field are mine.
12 If I were hungry, I' would not tell‿thee:
For the world is' mine, and the‿fulness there-of.
13 Will I eat the' flesh of bulls,
Or' drink the blood of goats?
14 Offer unto' God thanks-giving;
And pay thy' vows un-to the‿Most High:
15 And call upon me in the' day of trouble:
I will deliver thee, and' thou shalt glori-fy me.
16 But unto the wicked God saith, What hast thou to do to de'clare my statutes,
Or that thou shouldest take my' cove-nant in thy mouth?
17 Seeing thou' hatest in-struction,
And' castest my words be-hind‿thee.
18 When thou sawest a thief, then thou con'sent-edst with‿him,
And hast been par'ta-ker with a-dulterers.
19 Thou givest thy' mouth to evil,
And thy' tongue frameth de-ceit.

PSALMS.

20 Thou sittest and speakest a'gainst thy brother;
 Thou' slanderest thine own mother's son.
21 These things hast thou done, and I kept silence;
  thou thoughtest that I was altogether such an
  one' as thy-self:
 But I will reprove thee, and set them in' order
  be-fore thine eyes.
22 Now consider this, ye that for'gët God,
 Lest I tear you in pieces, and there be' nöne to
  de-liver.
23 Whoso offereth praise' glori-fieth me:
 And to him that ordereth his conversation aright
  will I' shew the⌣sal-vation of God.

PSALM LI.

¶ To the chief Musician, A Psalm of David, when Nathan the prophet came unto him, after he had gone in to Bath-sheba.

HAVE mercy upon me, O God, according to' thy
  loving-kindness:
 According unto the multitude of thy tender mercies' blot out my trans-gressions.
2 Wash me throughly from' mine in-iquity,
 And' cleanse me from my sin.
3 For I acknowledge' my trans-gressions:
 And my' sin is ever be-fore⌣me.
4 Against thee, thee only, have I sinned, and done
  this evil' in thy sight:
 That thou mightest be justified when thou speakest,
  and be' clëar when thou judgest.
5 Behold, I was shapen' in in-iquity;
 And in' sin did my⌣mother con-ceive⌣me.
6 Behold, thou desirest truth in the' in-ward parts:
 And in the hidden part thou shalt' make me
  to⌣knöw wisdom.
7 Purge me with hyssop, and I' shall be clean:
 Wash me, and I' shall be whiter than snow.

61

PSALMS.

8 Make me to hear' joy and gladness;
   That the bones which thou hast' bro-ken may re-joice.
9 Hide thy face' from my sins,
   And blot' out all mine in-iquities.
10 Create in me a clean' heart, O God;
   And re'new a right spirit with-in me.
11 Cast me not away' from thy presence;
   And take not thy' ho-ly spi-rit from me.
12 Restore unto me the joy of' thy sal-vation;
   And up'hold me with thy free spirit.
13 Then will I teach trans'gressors thy ways;
   And sinners shall' be con-verted un-to thee.
14 Deliver me from bloodguiltiness, O God, thou God of' my sal-vation:
   And my tongue shall sing a'löud of thy righteousness.
15 O LORD, open' thou my lips;
   And my mouth shall' shëw forth thy praise.
16 For thou desirest not sacrifice; else' would I give it:
   Thou delightest' not in bürnt offering.
17 The sacrifices of God are a' bro-ken spirit:
   A broken and a contrite heart, O God', thou wilt not de-spise.
18 Do good in thy good pleasure' un-to Zion:
   Build' thou the walls of Jerusalem.
19 Then shalt thou be pleased with the sacrifices of righteousness, with burnt offering and' whole burnt offering:
   Then shall they offer' bullocks up-on thine altar.

PSALM LII.

¶ To the chief Musician, Maschil, A Psalm of David, when Doeg the Edomite came and told Saul, and said unto him, David is come to the house of Ahimelech.

WHY boastest thou thyself in mischief', O mighty man?
The goodness of' God en-dureth con-tinually.

PSALMS.

2 Thy tongue de'vis-eth mischiefs;
Like a sharp' ra-zor, working de-ceitfully.
3 Thou lovest evil' more than good;
And lying' rather than to‿spëak righteousness. Selah.
4 Thou lovest all de'vour-ing words,
O' thou de-ceit-ful tongue.
5 God shall likewise destroy' thee for ever;
He shall take thee away, and pluck thee out of thy dwelling place, and root thee' out of the‿land of the‿living. Selah.
6 The righteous also shall' see, and fear,
And' shäll laugh at him:
7 Lo, this is the man that made not' God his strength;
But trusted in the abundance of his riches, and' strengthened him-self in‿his wickedness.
8 But I am like a green olive tree in the' house of God:
I trust in the mercy of' God for ever and ever.
9 I will praise thee for ever, because' thou hast done‿it:
And I will wait on thy name; for it is' good be-fore thy saints.

PSALM LIII.

¶ To the chief Musician upon Mahalath, Maschil, A Psalm of David.

THE fool hath said in his heart, There is' nö God.
Corrupt are they, and have done abominable iniquity: there is' none that do-eth good.
2 God looked down from heaven upon the' children of men,
To see if there were any that did under'stand, that did seek God.
3 Every one of them is gone back: they are altogether be'cöme filthy;
There is none that doeth' göod, no, not one.

PSALMS.

4 Have the workers of in'iquity no knowledge?
 Who eat up my people as they eat bread: they'
  have not called upon God.
5 There were they in great fear, where no fear was:
  for God hath scattered the bones of him that
  en'campeth a-gainst_thee:
 Thou hast put them to shame, be'cause God hath
  de-spised_them.
6 Oh that the salvation of Israel were come' out of
  Zion!
 When God bringeth back the captivity of his people,
  Jacob shall rejoice, and' Is-rael shall be glad.

PSALM LIV.

¶ To the chief Musician on Neginoth, Maschil, A Psalm of David, when the Ziphims came and said to Saul, Doth not David hide himself with us?

SAVE me, O God', by thy name,
 And' judge me by thy strength.
2 Hear my' prayer, O God;
 Give ear to the' words of my mouth.
3 For strangers are risen up against me, and oppres-
  sors seek' after my soul:
 They' have_not set God be-fore_them. Selah.
4 Behold, God' is mine helper:
 The LORD is with' them that uphold my soul.
5 He shall reward evil' unto mine enemies:
 Cut' them off in thy truth.
6 I will freely sacrifice' un-to thee:
 I will praise thy name, O' LORD, for it is good.
7 For he hath delivered me' out of_all trouble:
 And mine eye hath seen his de'sire up-on mine
  enemies.

PSALMS.

PSALM LV.

¶ To the chief Musician on Neginoth, Maschil, A Psalm of David.

GIVE ear to my' prayer, O God;
And hide not thyself' from my sup-pli-cation.
2 Attend unto' me, and hear_me:
I mourn in my com'plaint, and make a noise;
3 Because of the voice of the enemy, because of the
   op'pression of the_wicked:
For they cast iniquity upon me', and in wrath
   they hate_me.
4 My heart is sore' pained with-in_me:
And the terrors of' death are fallen up-on_me.
5 Fearfulness and trembling are' come up-on_me,
And' horror hath o-ver-whelmed_me.
6 And I said, O that I had' wings like a_dove!
For then would I fly a'way, and be at rest.
7 Lo, then would I' wander far off,
And re'main in the wilderness. Selah.
8 I would' hasten my escape
From the' win-dy storm and tempest.
9 Destroy, O LORD, and di'vide their tongues:
For I have seen' violence and strife in the_city.
10 Day and night they go about it upon tho' walls
   there-of:
Mischief also and sorrow' are in the_midst of it.
11 Wickedness is in the' midst there-of:
Deceit and guile de'part not from her streets.
12 For it was not an enemy that reproached me; then
   I' could have borne_it:
Neither was it he that hated me that did magnify
   himself against me; then I would have' hid
   my-self from_him:
13 But it was thou, a' man mine equal,
My' guide, and mine ac-quaintance.
14 We took sweet' counsel to-gether,
And walked unto the' house of God in company.

PSALMS.

15 Let death seize upon them, and let them go down'
quick into hell:
For wickedness is in their' dwell-ings, and a-mong‿them.
16 As for me, I will' call upon God;
A'nd the LORD shall save‿me.
17 Evening, and morning, and at noon, will I pray,
and' cry a-loud:
And' he shall hear my voice.
18 He hath delivered my soul in peace from the battle
that' was a-gainst‿me:
For' there were ma-ny with‿me.
19 God shall hear, and afflict them, even he that
a'bideth of old. Selah.
Because they have no changes', therefore they fear
not God.
20 He hath put forth his hands against such as be at'
peace with him:
He' häth broken his covenant.
21 The words of his mouth were smoother than but-ter, but war was' in his heart:
His words were softer than oil, yet' were they
dräwn swords.
22 Cast thy burden upon the LORD, and he' shall sus-tain‿thee:
He shall never suffer the' right-eous to be moved.
23 But thou, O God, shalt bring them down into the'
pit of destruction:
Bloody and deceitful men shall not live out half
their days; but' I will trust in thee.

PSALM LVI.

¶ To the chief Musician upon Jonath-elem-rechokim, Michtam
of David, when the Philistines took him in Gath.

BE merciful unto me, O God: for man would'
swallow me up;
He' fight-ing daily op-presseth‿me.

2 Mine enemies would daily' swallow me up:
  For they be many that fight a'gainst me, O thou
    Most High.
3 What time I' am a-fraid,
  I' will trust in thee.
4 In God I will praise his word, in God I have' put
    my trust;
  I will not fear what' flesh can do un-to me.
5 Every day they' wrest my words:
  All their thoughts are a'gainst me for evil.
6 They gather them'selves to-gether,
  They hide them-selves, they mark my steps, when
    they' wait for my soul.
7 Shall they escape' by in-iquity?
  In thine anger cast' down the people, O God.
8 Thou' tellest my wanderings:
  Put thou my tears into thy bottle: are' they not
    in thy book?
9 When I cry unto thee, then shall mine' enemies
    turn back:
  This I' know; for God is for me.
10 In God will I' praise his word:
  In the LORD' will I praise his word.
11 In God have I' put my trust:
  I will not be afraid what' man can do un to me.
12 Thy vows are upon' me, O God:
  I will render' prais-es un-to thee.
13 For thou hast delivered my' soul from death:
  Wilt not thou deliver my feet from falling, that I
    may walk before God in the' light of the living?

PSALM LVII.

¶ To the chief Musician, Al-taschith, Michtam of David, when
he fled from Saul in the cave.

BE merciful unto me, O God, be merciful unto me:
  for my soul' trusteth in thee:
Yea, in the shadow of thy wings will I make my
  refuge, until these ca'lamities be o-ver-past.

PSALMS.

2 I will cry unto' God Most High;
  Unto God that per'form-eth all things for_me.
3 He shall send from heaven, and save me from the reproach of him that would' swallow me up. Selah.
  God shall send forth his' mer-cy and his truth.
4 My soul is among lions: and I lie even among them that are' set on fire,
  Even the sons of men, whose teeth are spears and arrows, and their' tongue a shärp sword.
5 Be thou exalted, O God, a'bove the heavens;
  Let thy glory be a'böve all the earth.
6 They have prepared a net for my steps; my soul is' bow-ed down:
  They have digged a pit before me, into the midst whereof' they are fallen them-selves. Selah.
7 My heart is' fixed, O God,
  My heart is fixed: I will' sĭng and give praise.
8 Awake up, my glory; awake', psaltery and harp:
  I my'self will awäke early.
9 I will praise thee, O LORD, a'mong the people:
  I will sing unto' thee a-mong the nations.
10 For thy mercy is great' unto the heavens,
  And thy' truth un-to the clouds.
11 Be thou exalted, O God, a'bove the heavens:
  Let thy glory be a'böve all the earth.

PSALM LVIII.

¶ To the chief Musician, Al-taschith, Michtam of David.

DO ye indeed speak righteousness', O congre-gation?
  Do ye judge uprightly', O ye sons of men?
2 Yea, in heart ye' wörk wickedness;
  Ye weigh the violence' of your hands in the_earth.
3 The wicked are estranged' from the womb:
  They go astray as soon as they be' börn, speak-ing lies.

PSALMS.

4 Their poison is like the' poison of a serpent:
 They are like the deaf' adder that stoppeth her ear;
5 Which will not hearken to the' voice of charmers,
 Cha'rm-ing never so wisely.
6 Break their teeth, O God', in their mouth:
 Break out the great teeth of the' yöung lions, O LORD.
7 Let them melt away as waters which' run continually:
 When he bendeth his bow to shoot his arrows, let them' be as cut in pieces.
8 As a snail which melteth, let every one of them' pass a-way:
 Like the untimely birth of a woman, that they' may not see the sun.
9 Before your pots can' feel the thorns,
 He shall take them away as with a whirlwind, both' living, and in his wrath.
10 The righteous shall rejoice when he' seeth the vengeance:
 He shall wash his feet in the' blöod of the wicked.
11 So that a man shall say, Verily, there is a re'ward for the righteous:
 Verily, he is a God that' judg-eth in the earth.

PSALM LIX.

¶ To the chief Musician, Al-taschith, Michtam of David, when Saul sent, and they watched the house to kill him.

DELIVER me from mine enemies', O my God:
 Defend me from them that' rïse up a-gainst me.
2 Deliver me from the workers' of in-iquity,
 And' save me from blood-y men.

PSALMS.

3 For, lo, they lie in wait' for my soul:
The mighty are gathered. against me; not for my transgression, nor' for my sin, O LORD.
4 They run and prepare themselves with'out my fault:
Awake to' help me, and be-hold.
5 Thou, therefore, O LORD God of hosts, the God of Israel, awake to visit' all the heathen:
Be not merciful to' a-ny wicked trans-gressors. Selah.
6 They re'turn at evening:
They make a noise like a dog, and go' round a-bout the city.
7 Behold, they belch out' with their mouth:
Swords are in their lips: for' who, say they, doth hear?
8 But thou, O LORD, shalt' laugh at them;
Thou shalt have all the' hea-then in de-rision.
9 Because of his strength will I' wait upon thee:
For' God is my de-fence.
10 The God of my mercy' shall pre-vent me:
God shall let me see my de'sire up-on mine enemies.
11 Slay them not, lest my' people for-get:
Scatter them by thy power; and bring them' down, O LORD our shield.
12 For the sin of their mouth, and the words of their lips, let them even be taken' in their pride:
And for cursing and' ly-ing which they speak.
13 Consume them in wrath, consume them, that they' may not be:
And let them know that God ruleth in Jacob' unto the ends of the earth. Selah.
14 And at evening' let them re-turn;
And let them make a noise like a dog, and go' round a-bout the city.
15 Let them wander up and' down for meat,
And grudge' if they be not satisfied.

PSALMS.

16 But I will sing of thy power; yea, I will sing aloud
of thy mercy′ in the morning:
For thou hast been my defence and refuge in the′
däy of my trouble.
17 Unto thee, O my strength′, will I sing:
For God is my defence′, and the Göd of my mercy.

PSALM LX.

¶ To the chief Musician upon Shushan-eduth, Michtam of David, to teach; when he strove with Aram-naharaim and with Aram-zobah, when Joab returned, and smote of Edom in the Valley of Salt twelve thousand.

O GOD, thou hast cast us off, thou hast scattered us, thou hast′ been dis-pleased;
O turn thy′self to us a-gain.
2 Thou hast made the earth to tremble′: thou hast broken it:
Heal the breaches′ there-of; for it shaketh.
3 Thou hast showed thy′ people hard things:
Thou hast made us to′ drink the wine of astonishment.
4 Thou hast given a banner to′ them that feared thee,
That it may be displayed be′cäuse of the truth.
Selah.
5 That thy beloved may′ be de-livered:
Save with′ thy right hand, and hear me.
6 God hath spoken′ in his holiness;
I will rejoice, I will divide Shechem, and mete′ out the valley of Succoth.
7 Gilead is mine, and Ma′nasseh is mine:
Ephraim also is the strength of mine head′; Ju-dah is my lawgiver;
8 Moab is my washpot: over Edom will I cast′ out my shoe;
Philistia, triumph′ thou be-cause of me.
9 Who will bring me in′to the strong city?
Who will′ lead me in-to Edom?

PSALMS.

10 Wilt not thou, O God, which hadst' cast us off?
And thou, O God, which didst not' go out with our armies?
11 Give us' help from trouble:
For' vain is the‿help of man.
12 Through God we' shall do valiantly:
For he it is that shall' trëad down our enemies.

PSALM LXI.

¶ To the chief Musician upon Neginah, A Psalm of David.

HEAR my' cry, O God;
At'tend un-to my prayer.
2 From the end of the earth will I cry unto thee,
when my heart is' o-ver-whelmed:
Lead me to the rock' that is higher than I.
3 For thou hast been a' shel-ter for‿me,
And a' strong tower from the enemy.
4 I will abide in thy' tabernacle for ever:
I will trust in the' co-vert of thy wings.   Selah.
5 For thou, O God, hast' heard my vows:
Thou hast given me the heritage of' those that fear thy name.
6 Thou wilt pro'long the‿king's life:
And his' years as many gene-rations.
7 He shall abide before' God for ever:
O prepare mercy and' truth, which may pre-serve‿him.
8 So will I sing praise unto thy' name for ever,
That I may' daily per-form my vows.

PSALM LXII.

¶ To the chief Musician, to Jeduthun, A Psalm of David.

TRULY my soul' waiteth upon God:
From' him cometh my sal-vation.
2 He only is my rock and' my sal-vation;
He is my defence; I shall' not be great-ly moved.

PSALMS.

3 How long will ye imagine mischief a'gainst a man?
Ye shall be slain, all of you: as a bowing wall shall ye be, and' as a totter-ing fence.
4 They only consult to cast him down' from his excellency:
They delight in lies: they bless with their' mouth, but they curse inwardly. Selah.
5 My soul, wait thou' only upon God;
For my expec'ta-tion is from him.
6 He only is my rock and' my sal-vation:
He is my defence'; I shall not be moved.
7 In God is my salvation' and my glory:
The rock of my strength, and my' re-fuge, is in God.
8 Trust in him at all times; ye people, pour out your' heart be-fore͜him:
God' is a re-fuge for͜us. Selah.
9 Surely men of low degree are vanity, and men of high degree' are a lie:
To be laid in the balance, they are alto'ge-ther lighter than vanity.
10 Trust not in oppression, and become not' vain in robbery:
If riches increase', set͜not your heart up-on͜them.
11 God hath' spok-en once:
Twice have I heard this; that power be'long-eth un-to God.
12 Also unto thee, O Lord, be'long-eth mercy:
For thou renderest to every man ac'cord-ing to his work.

PSALM LXIII.

¶ A Psalm of David, when he was in the wilderness of Judah.

O GOD, thou art my God; early' will I seek͜thee:
My soul thirsteth for thee, my flesh longeth for thee in a dry and thirsty land', where no wa-ter is;

PSALMS.

2 To see thy power' and thy glory,
So as I have' seen thee in the sanctuary.
3 Because thy lovingkindness is' better than life,
My' lips shall praise thee.
4 Thus will I bless thee' while I live:
I will lift up my' hands in thy name.
5 My soul shall be satisfied as with' marrow and fatness;
And my mouth shall' praise␣thee with joy-ful lips:
6 When I remember thee up'on my bed,
And meditate on' thee in the␣night watches.
7 Because thou hast' been my help,
Therefore in the shadow of thy' wings will I re-joice.
8 My soul followeth' hard after thee:
Thy' right hand up-holdeth␣me.
9 But those that seek my' soul to destroy␣it,
Shall go into the' low-er parts of the␣earth.
10 They shall' fall by the␣sword;
They shall' be a portion for foxes.
11 But the king shall rejoice in God; every one that sweareth by' him shall glory:
But the mouth of them that' speak lies shall be stopped.

PSALM LXIV.

¶ To the chief Musician, A Psalm of David.

HEAR my voice, O God', in my prayer:
Preserve my' life from fear of the␣enemy.
2 Hide me from the secret' counsel of the␣wicked;
From the insurrection of the' work-ers of in-iquity:
3 Who whet their' tongue like a␣sword,
And bend their bows to shoot their arrows', ev-en bit-ter words:
4 That they may shoot in secret' at the perfect:
Suddenly do they' shoot at him, and fear␣not.

PSALMS.

5 They encourage themselves in an' e-vil matter:
 They commune of laying snares privily'; they say,
 Who shall see⌣them?
6 They search out iniquities; they accomplish a'
 dili-gent search:
 Both the inward thought of every one of them',
 and the heart, is deep.
7 But God shall shoot at them' with an arrow;
 Suddenly' shäll they be wounded.
8 So they shall make their own tongue to fall up'on
 them-selves:
 All that' see⌣them shall flee a-way.
9 And all men shall fear, and shall declare the' work
 of God;
 For they shall wisely con'si-der of his doing.
10 The righteous shall be glad in the LORD, and shall'
 trust in him;
 And all the' upright in heart shall glory.

PSALM LXV.

¶ To the chief Musician, A Psalm and Song of David.

PRAISE waiteth for thee, O' God, in Zion:
 And unto thee' shall the⌣vow be per-formed.
2 O thou that' hear-est prayer,
 Unto' thee shall all flesh come.
3 Iniquities pre'vail a-gainst⌣me:
 As for our transgressions', thou shalt purge them
 away.
4 Blessed is the man whom thou choosest, and caus-
 est to approach unto thee, that he may' dwell⌣in
 thy courts:
 We shall be satisfied with the goodness of thy
 house, even' of thy ho-ly temple.
5 By terrible things in righteousness wilt thou
 answer us, O God of' our sal-vation;
 Who art the confidence of all the ends of the earth,
 and of them that are afar' off up-on the sea:

PSALMS.

6 Which by his strength setteth' fast the mountains;
 B'e-ing girded with power:
7 Which stilleth the' noise of the‿seas,
 The noise of their waves, and the' tu-mult of the people.
8 They also that dwell in the uttermost parts are' afraid at‿thy tokens:
 Thou makest the outgoings of the morning and' even-ing to re-joice.
9 Thou visitest the earth, and waterest it: thou greatly enrichest it with the river of God, which is' full of water:
 Thou preparest them corn, when thou hast' so pro-vid-ed for‿it.
10 Thou waterest the ridges thereof abundantly: thou settlest the' furrows there-of:
 Thou makest it soft with showers: thou' blessest the springing there-of.
11 Thou crownest the year' with thy goodness:
 And' thy paths drop fatness.
12 They drop upon the' pastures of the‿wilderness:
 And the little hills re'joice on ev-ery side.
13 The pastures are' clothed with flocks;
 The valleys also are covered over with corn; they shout for' joy, they al-so sing.

PSALM LXVI.

¶ To the chief Musician, A Song or Psalm.

MAKE a joyful noise' un-to God,
 A'·ll ye lands:
2 Sing forth the' honour of‿his name;
 M'äke his praise glorious.
3 Say unto God, How terrible art thou' in thy works!
 Through the greatness of thy power shall thine enemies sub'mit them-selves un-to‿thee.

PSALMS.

4 All the earth shall worship thee, and shall' sing un-to‿thee;
   They shall' sïng to thy name.   Selah.
5 Come and see the' works of God:
   He is terrible in his doing' toward the children of men.
6 He turned the sea into dry land: they went through the' flood on foot:
   There did' we re-joice in him.
7 He ruleth by his power for ever; his eyes be'hold the nations:
   Let not the re'bellious ex-alt them-selves.   Selah.
8 O bless our' God, ye people,
   And make the voice of his' präise to be heard:
9 Which holdeth our' soul in life,
   And suffereth not our' feet to be moved.
10 For thou, O' God, hast proved‿us:
    Thou hast' tried‿us, as silver is tried.
11 Thou broughtest us' into the net;
    Thou laidst af'fliction up-on our loins.
12 Thou hast caused men to ride over our heads: we went through' fire and‿through water;
    But thou broughtest us out' in-to a‿wealth-y place.
13 I will go into thy house with' bürnt-offerings:
    I' will pay thee my vows,
14 Which my' lips have uttered,
    And my mouth hath spoken', when I was in trouble.
15 I will offer unto thee burnt sacrifices of fatlings, with the' incense of rams;
    I will' of-fer bullocks with goats.   Selah.
16 Come and hear, all' ye that‿fear God,
    And I will declare what he' hath done for my soul.
17 I cried unto him' with my mouth,
    And he was ex'toll-ed with my tongue.
18 If I regard iniquity' in my heart,
    The' Lörd will not hear‿me:

PSALMS.

19 But verily' God hath heard⌣me;
 He hath attended to the' vöice of my prayer.
20 Blessed be God, which hath not turned' away my prayer,
 N'or his mer-cy from⌣me.

PSALM LXVII.

¶ To the chief Musician on Neginoth, A Psalm or Song.

GOD be merciful unto' us, and bless⌣us;
 And cause his' face to shine up-on⌣us. Selah.
2 That thy way may be' known upon earth,
 Thy saving' health a-mong all nations.
3 Let the people' praise⌣thee, O God;
 Let' all the peo-ple praise⌣thee.
4 O let the nations be glad and' sing for joy;
 For thou shalt judge the people righteously, and govern the' na-tions up-on earth. Selah.
5 Let the people' praise⌣thee, O God;
 Let' all the peo-ple praise⌣thee.
6 Then shall the earth' yield her increase;
 And God, even' our own God, shall bless⌣us.
7 God' shäll bless⌣us;
 And all the' ends of the⌣earth shall fear⌣him.

PSALM LXVIII.

¶ To the chief Musician, A Psalm or Song of David.

LET God arise, let his' enemies be scattered:
 Let them also that' hate him flee be-fore⌣him.
2 As smoke is driven away, so' drive them away;
 As wax melteth before the fire, so let the wicked' perish in the⌣presence of God.
3 But let the righteous be glad; let them rejoice be'före God:
 Yea', let⌣them ex-ceedingly re-joice.

PSALMS.

4 Sing unto God, sing' praises to his name:
Extol him that rideth upon the heavens by his name JAH', and re-joice be-fore him.
5 A father of the fatherless, and a' judge of the widows,
Is' God in his holy habi-tation.
6 God setteth the solitary in families: he bringeth out those which are' bound with chains:
But the re'bellious dwell in a dry land.
7 O God, when thou wentest forth be'fore thy people,
When thou didst' march through the wilderness; Selah:
8 The earth shook, the heavens also dropped at the' presence of God:
Even Sinai itself was moved at the presence of God, the God of Israel.
9 Thou, O God, didst send a' plenti-ful rain,
Whereby thou didst confirm thine in'heritance, when it was weary.
10 Thy congregation hath' dwelt there-in:
Thou, O God, hast prepared of thy' good-ness for the poor.
11 The LORD' gave the word:
Great was the' company of those that published it.
12 Kings of armies did' flee a-pace:
And she that tarried at' home di-vided the spoil.
13 Though ye have lien a'mong the pots,
Yet shall ye be as the wings of a dove covered with silver, and her' feathers with yel-low gold.
14 When the Almighty scattered' kings in it,
It was' white as snow in Salmon.
15 The hill of God is as the' hill of Bashan;
An high hill', as the hill of Bashan.
16 Why leap ye, ye high hills? this is the hill which God de'sireth to dwell in;
Yea, the LORD will' dwell in it for ever.

PSALMS.

17 The chariots of God are twenty thousand, even'
thousands of angels :
The LORD is among them, as in Sinai', in the ho-ly
place.
18 Thou hast ascended on high, thou hast led captivity captive; thou hast received' gifts for men;
Yea, for the rebellious also, that the LORD' God
might dwell a-mong_them.
19 Blessed be the LORD, who daily loadeth' us with
benefits,
Even the' God of our sal-vation. Selah.
20 He that is our God is the' God of_sal-vation;
And unto God the LORD be' long the issues from death.
21 But God shall wound the' head of_his enemies,
And the hairy scalp of such an one as goeth' on
still in his trespasses.
22 The LORD said, I will bring a'gain from Bashan,
I will bring my people again' from the depths
of the_sea:
23 That thy foot may be dipped in the' blood of_thine
enemies,
And the tongue' of thy dogs in the_same.
24 They have seen thy' goings, O God;
Even the goings of my God, my' King, in the
sanctuary.
25 The singers went before, the players on instruments'
follow-ed after;
Among them were the' dam-sels playing with
timbrels.
26 Bless ye God in the' con-gre-gations,
Even the LORD', from the fountain of Israel.
27 There is little Benjamin with their ruler, the princes
of Judah' and their council,
The princes of Zebulun', and the princes of
Naphtali.
28 Thy God hath com'manded thy strength:
Strengthen, O God, that' which thou hast wrought
for_us.

PSALMS.

29 Because of thy' temple at Jerusalem
 Shall' kings bring presents un-to‿thee.
30 Rebuke the company of spearmen, the multitude
    of the bulls, with the' calves of the‿people,
 Till every one submit himself with pieces of silver:
    scatter thou the people' that de-light in war.
31 Princes shall come' out of Egypt;
 Ethiopia shall soon stretch' out her hands unto God.
32 Sing unto God, ye' kingdoms of the‿earth;
 O sing'ıpraises un-to the LORD; Selah:
33 To him that rideth upon the heavens of heavens,
    which' were of old;
 Lo, he doth send out his voice, and' that a might-y
    voice.
34 Ascribe ye' strength unto God:
 His excellency is over Israel, and his' strength is
    in the clouds.
35 O God, thou art terrible out of thy' ho-ly places:
 The God of Israel is he that giveth strength and
    power unto his' peo-ple. Blessed be God.

PSALM LXIX.

¶ To the chief Musician upon Shoshannim, A Psalm of David.

SAVE' me, O God;
 For the waters are' come in unto my soul.
2 I sink in deep mire, where there' is no standing:
 I am come into deep waters', where the floods
    over-flow‿me.
3 I am weary of my crying: my' throat is dried:
 Mine eyes fail while I' wäit for my God.
4 They that hate me without a cause are more than
    the' hairs of‿mine head:
 They that would destroy me, being mine enemies
    wrongfully, are mighty: then I restored that'
    which I took not away.
5 O God, thou' knowest my foolishness;
 And my sins' are not hid from thee.

F   81

PSALMS.

6 Let not them that wait on thee, O LORD God of hosts, be ashamed' for my sake:
Let not those that seek thee be confounded for my sake', Ö God of Israel.
7 Because for thy sake I have' borne re-proach;
Sh'ame hath covered my face.
8 I am become a stranger' unto my brethren,
And an alien' unto my mo-ther's children.
9 For the zeal of thine house hath' eaten me up;
And the reproaches of them that reproached' thee are fallen up-on‿me.
10 When I wept, and chastened my' soul with fasting, That' was to my re-proach.
11 I made sackcloth' also my garment:
And I be'came a pro-verb to‿them.
12 They that sit in the gate' speak a-gainst‿me;
And I' was the song of the‿drunkards.
13 But as for me, my prayer is unto thee, O LORD, in an' accept-able time:
O God, in the multitude of thy mercy, hear me, in the' truth of thy sal-vation.
14 Deliver me out of the mire, and' let‿me not sink:
Let me be delivered from them that hate me, and' out of the‿deep waters.
15 Let not the waterflood overflow me, neither let the deep' swallow me up,
And let not the pit' shut her mouth up-on‿me.
16 Hear me, O LORD; for thy loving'kindness is good:
Turn unto me according to the multitude' of thy ten-der mercies.
17 And hide not thy face' from thy servant;
For I am in' trou-ble: hear me speedily.
18 Draw nigh unto my soul', and re-deem‿it:
Deliver me be'cäuse of mine enemies.
19 Thou hast known my reproach, and my shame, and' my dis-honour:
Mine' adversaries are all be-fore‿thee.

PSALMS.

20 Reproach hath broken my heart; and I am' full of heaviness:
And I looked for some to take pity, but there was none; and for' comforters, but I found none.
21 They gave me also gall' for my meat;
And in my thirst they' gave me vinegar to drink.
22 Let their table become a' snare be-fore‿them;
And that which should have been for their welfare', let it become a trap.
23 Let their eyes be darkened', that they see‿not;
And make their' loins con-tinually to shake.
24 Pour out thine indig'nation up-on‿them,
And let thy wrathful' an-ger take hold of‿them.
25 Let their habi'tation be desolate;
And let' none dwell in their tents.
26 For they persecute him whom' thou hast smitten:
And they talk to the grief of' those whom thou hast wounded.
27 Add iniquity unto' their in-iquity;
And let them' not come into thy righteousness.
28 Let them be blotted out of the' book of the‿living,
And not be' writ-ten with the righteous.
29 But I am' poor and sorrowful:
Let thy salvation, O God', set me up on high.
30 I will praise the name of' God with a‿song,
And will' magni-fy him with thanksgiving.
31 This also shall' please the LORD
Better than an ox or bullock' that hath horns and hoofs.
32 The humble shall see this', and be glad:
And your heart shall' live that sëek God.
33 For the LORD' heareth the poor,
And de'spis-eth not his prisoners.
34 Let the heaven and' ëarth praise‿him,
The seas, and every' thing that moveth there-in.
35 For God will save Zion, and will build the' cities of Judah;
That they may dwell there, and' have it in pos-session.

PSALMS.

36 The seed also of his servants' shall in-herit͜ it:
And they that love his' name shall dwell there-in.

PSALM LXX.

¶ To the chief Musician, A Psalm of David, to bring to remembrance.

MAKE haste, O God', to de-liver͜ me;
Make' haste to help͜ me, O LORD.
2 Let them be ashamed and confounded that seek'
after my soul:
Let them be turned backward, and put to con-
fusion', that de-sire my hurt.
3 Let them be turned back for a reward' of their
shame,
That' say, A-ha, A-ha!
4 Let all those that seek thee rejoice and be' glad in
thee:
And let such as love thy salvation say con'tinually,
Let God be magnified.
5 But I am poor and needy; make haste unto' me,
O God:
Thou art my help and my deliverer; O' LÖRD,
make no tarrying.

PSALM LXXI.

IN thee, O LORD, do I' put my trust:
Let me' never be put to͜ con-fusion.
2 Deliver me in thy righteousness, and' cause͜ me
to͜ es-cape:
Incline thine' ear unto me, and save͜ me.
3 Be thou my strong habitation, whereunto I may
con'tinually re-sort:
Thou hast given commandment to save me; for
thou art my' röck and my fortress.

PSALMS.

4 Deliver me, O my God, out of the' hand of the‿wicked,
   Out of the hand of the un'righteous and cru-el man.
5 For thou art my hope', O LORD God:
   Thou art' my trust from my youth.
6 By thee have I been holden up from the womb:
   thou art he that took me out of my' mo-ther's bowels:
   My praise shall' be con-tinually of thee.
7 I am as a wonder' un-to many;
   But' thou art my strong refuge.
8 Let my mouth be filled' with thy praise
   And with thy' hon-our all the day.
9 Cast me not off in the' time of‿old age;
   Forsake me' not when my strength faileth.
10 For mine enemies' speak a-gainst‿me;
   And they that lay wait for my' soul take counsel to-gether,
11 Saying', God hath forsaken‿him:
   Persecute and take him; for there is' nōne to de-liver‿him.
12 O God, be not' fär from‿me:
   O my God, make' häste for my help.
13 Let them be confounded and consumed that are adversaries' to my soul;
   Let them be covered with reproach and dis'honour that seek my hurt.
14 But I will' hope con-tinually,
   And will yet' praise thee more and more.
15 My mouth shall show forth thy righteousness and thy salvation' all the day;
   For I' know not the‿numbers there-of.
16 I will go in the strength of the' LORD God:
   I will make mention of thy righteousness', even of thīne only.
17 O God, thou hast taught me' from my youth:
   And hitherto have I de'clared thy won-drous works.

PSALMS.

18 Now also when I am old and greyheaded, O God, for'sake me not;
Until I have showed thy strength unto this generation, and thy power to every' one that is to come.
19 Thy righteousness also, O God, is very high, who hast' done great things:
O God, who is' like un-to thee!
20 Thou, which hast showed me great and' sore troubles,
Shalt quicken me again, and shalt bring me up again' from the depths of the earth.
21 Thou shalt in'crease my greatness,
And' comfort me on ev-ery side.
22 I will also praise thee with the psaltery, even thy truth', O my God:
Unto thee will I sing with the harp, O thou' Ho-ly One of Israel.
23 My lips shall greatly rejoice when I' sing un-to thee;
And my soul, which' thou hast re-deemed.
24 My tongue also shall talk of thy righteousness' all the day long:
For they are confounded, for they are brought unto' shame, that seek my hurt.

PSALM LXXII.

¶ A Psalm for Solomon.

GIVE the king thy' judgments, O God,
And thy' righteousness un-to the king's son.
2 He shall judge thy' people with righteousness,
And' thy poor with judgment.
3 The mountains shall bring' peace to the people,
And the' lit-tle hills, by righteousness.
4 He shall judge the poor of the people, he shall save the' children of the needy,
And shall break in' pie-ces the op-pressor.

PSALMS.

5 They shall fear thee as long as the sun and' moon en-dure,
Through'out all ge-ne-rations.
6 He shall come down like rain up'on the‿mown grass:
As' showers that water the earth.
7 In his days shall the' right-eous flourish;
And abundance of peace so' long as the‿moon en-dureth.
8 He shall have dominion also from' sea to sea,
And from the river' unto the ends of the‿earth.
9 They that dwell in the wilderness shall' bow be-fore‿him:
And his' enemies shall lick the dust.
10 The kings of Tarshish and of the isles shall' bring presents:
The kings of Sheba and' Seba shall of-fer gifts.
11 Yea, all kings shall fall' down be-fore‿him:
All' nations shall serve him.
12 For he shall deliver the needy' when he crieth;
The poor also, and' him that hath no helper.
13 He shall spare the' poor and needy,
And shall' save the souls of the‿needy.
14 He shall redeem their soul from' deceit and violence:
And precious shall their' blood be in his sight.
15 And he shall live, and to him shall be given of the' gold of Sheba:
Prayer also shall be made for him continually; and' daily shall he be praised.
16 There shall be an handful of corn in the earth upon the' top of the‿mountains;
The fruit thereof shall shake like Lebanon: and they of the city shall' flourish like grass of the‿earth.
17 His name shall endure for ever: his name shall be continued as' long as the‿sun:
And men shall be blessed in him: all' nations shall call him Blessed.

PSALMS.

18 Blessed be the LORD God, the' God of Israel,
   Who' only doeth won-drous things.
19 And blessed be his glorious' name for ever:
   And let the whole earth be filled with his glory:
   A'mën, and A-men.
20 The' prayers of David
   The' son of Jesse are ended.

PSALM LXXIII.

¶ A Psalm of Asaph.

TRULY God is' good to Israel,
   Even to such as' are of a clëan heart.
2 But as for me, my feet were' al-most gone;
   My' steps had well nigh slipped.
3 For I was envious' at the foolish,
   When I' saw the pro-sperity of the wicked.
4 For there are no bands' in their death:
   But' thëir strength is firm.
5 They are not in trouble as' oth-er men;
   Neither are they' plagued like oth-er men.
6 Therefore pride compasseth them' about as a chain;
   Violence' covereth them as a garment.
7 Their eyes stand' out with fatness:
   They have' more than heart could wish.
8 They' are cor-rupt,
   And speak wickedly concerning op'pres-sion: they speak loftily.
9 They set their mouth a'gainst the heavens,
   And their' tongue walketh through the earth.
10 Therefore his people re'türn hither:
    And waters of a full' cup are wrung out to them.
11 And they say', How doth God know?
    And is there' know-ledge in the Most High?
12 Behold, these are the ungodly, who' prosper in the world;
    Th'ey in-crease in riches.

PSALMS.

13 Verily I have cleansed my' heart in vain,
And' washed my hands in innocency.
14 For all the day long have' I been plagued,
And' chasten-ed ev-ery morning.
15 If I say, I' will speak thus;
Behold, I should offend against the gene'ra-tion of thy children.
16 When I thought to' knöw this,
It' was too pain-ful for˷me;
17 Until I went into the' sanctuary of God;
Then' under-stood I their end.
18 Surely thou didst set them in' slip-pery places:
Thou castedst them' döwn into de-struction.
19 How are they brought into desolation', as in a˷moment!
They are' utterly con-sumed with terrors.
20 As a dream when' one a-waketh;
So, O LORD, when thou awakest, thou' shalt de-spise their image.
21 Thus my' heart was grieved,
And I was' prick-ed in my reins.
22 So foolish was' I, and ignorant:
I was' as a beast be-fore˷thee.
23 Nevertheless I am con'tinually with thee:
Thou hast holden' me by my right hand.
24 Thou shalt guide me' with thy counsel,
And afterward re'cëive me to glory.
25 Whom have I in' heaven but thee?
And there is none upon earth that' I de-sire be-side˷thee.
26 My flesh and my' hëart faileth:
But God is the strength of my heart', and my portion for ever.
27 For, lo, they that are far from' thee shall perish:
Thou hast destroyed all them that' go a-whoring from thee.
28 But it is good for me to draw' near to God:
I have put my trust in the LORD God, that I may de'cläre all thy works.

PSALM LXXIV.

¶ Maschil of Asaph.

O GOD, why hast thou cast us' off for ever?
Why doth thine anger smoke a'gainst the͜ sheep of thy pasture?
2 Remember thy congregation, which thou hast purchased of old; the rod of thine inheritance, which thou' hast re-deemed;
This mount Zion', where-in thou hast dwelt.
3 Lift up thy feet unto the per'petual deso-lations;
Even all that the enemy hath done' wicked-ly in the sanctuary.
4 Thine enemies roar in the midst of thy' con-gre-gations;
They set' up their ensigns for signs.
5 A' man was famous
According as he had lifted up' axes up-on the͜ thick trees;
6 But now they break down the' carved work thereof
At' once with axes and hammers.
7 They have cast fire' into thy sanctuary,
They have defiled by casting down the dwelling-place of' thy name to the ground.
8 They said in their hearts, Let us' destroy them together:
They have burned up all the' synagogues of God in the͜ land.
9 We see not our signs: there is no' more any prophet:
Neither is there among us' any that knoweth how long.
10 O God, how long shall the' adversary re-proach?
Shall the enemy blas'pheme thy name for ever?

11 Why withdrawest thou thy hand', even thy right‿hand?
Pluck' it out of thy bosom.
12 For God is my' King of old,
Working salvation' in the midst of the‿earth.
13 Thou didst divide the sea' by thy strength:
Thou brakest the heads of the' dra-gons in the waters.
14 Thou brakest the heads of le'viathan in pieces,
And gavest him to be meat to the' people inhabiting the wilderness.
15 Thou didst cleave the fountain' and the flood:
Thou' driedst up might-y rivers.
16 The day is thine, the night' also is thine:
Thou hast prepared the' light and the sun.
17 Thou hast set all the' borders of the‿earth:
Thou' hast made summer and winter.
18 Remember this, that the enemy hath re'proached, O Lord,
And that the foolish people' have blas-phemed thy name.
19 O deliver not the soul of thy turtledove unto the' multitude of the‿wicked:
Forget not the congregation' of thy poor for ever.
20 Have respect' unto the covenant;
For the dark places of the earth are full of the' ha-bi-tations of cruelty.
21 O let not the oppressed re'turn a-shamed:
Let the poor and' need-y praise thy name.
22 Arise, O God, plead' thine own cause:
Remember how the foolish' man re-proacheth thee daily.
23 Forget not the voice' of thine enemies:
The tumult of those that rise up against' thee increaseth con-tinually.

PSALMS.

PSALM LXXV.

¶ To the chief Musician, Al-taschith, A Psalm or Song of Asaph.

UNTO thee, O God, do we give thanks, unto thee
do' we give thanks:
For that thy name is near, thy' won-drous works
de-clare.
2 When I shall receive the' con-gre-gation,
I' will judge up-rightly.
3 The earth and all the inhabitants thereof' are dis-
solved:
I bear' up the pillars of it. Selah.
4 I said unto the fools', Deal not foolishly:
And to the wicked', Lift not up the horn:
5 Lift not up your' horn on high:
Sp'eak not with a stiff neck.
6 For promotion cometh' neither from the east,
Nor from the' west, nor from the south.
7 But' God is the judge:
He putteth down one, and' set-teth up an-other.
8 For in the hand of the LORD there is a cup, and the
wine is red; it is full of mixture; and he
poureth' out of the same:
But the dregs thereof, all the wicked of the earth
shall' wring them out, and drink them.
9 But I will de'clare for ever;
I will sing' praises to the God of Jacob.
10 All the horns of the wicked also will' I cut off;
But the horns of the' righteous shall be ex-alted.

PSALM LXXVI.

¶ To the chief Musician on Neginoth, A Psalm or Song of Asaph.

IN Judah' is God known:
His' name is great in Israel.

PSALMS.

2 In Salem also' is his tabernacle,
And his' dwell-ing place in Zion.
3 There brake he the' arrows of the⌣bow,
The shield, and the' swörd, and the battle.   Selah.
4 Thou art more' glorious and excellent
Th'an the mountains of prey.
5 The stout-hearted are spoiled, they have' slept their sleep:
And none of the men of' might have found their hands.
6 At thy rebuke, O' God of Jacob,
Both the chariot and horse are' cast in-to a⌣dead sleep.
7 Thou, even thou, art' to be feared:
And who may stand in thy sight when' önce thou art angry?
8 Thou didst cause judgment to be' heard from heaven;
The earth' fear-ed, and was still,
9 When God a'rose to judgment,
To save' all the meek of the⌣earth.   Selah.
10 Surely the wrath of' man shall praise⌣thee:
The remainder of' wrath shalt thou re-strain.
11 Vow, and pay unto the' LORD your God:
Let all that be round about him bring presents unto him that' ought to be feared.
12 He shall cut off the' spirit of princes:
He is' terrible to the⌣kings of the⌣earth.

PSALM LXXVII.

¶ To the chief Musician, to Jeduthun, A Psalm of Asaph.

I CRIED unto God' with my voice,
Even unto God with my voice; and' he gave ear un-to⌣me.
2 In the day of my trouble I' sought the LORD:
My sore ran in the night, and ceased not: my soul re'fus-ed to be comforted.

PSALMS.

3 I remembered God', and was troubled:
 I complained, and my' spirit was o-ver-whelmed. Selah.
4 Thou holdest mine' eyes waking:
 I am so troubled' that I can-not speak.
5 I have considered the' days of old,
 The' years of an-cient times.
6 I call to remembrance my' song in the‿night:
 I commune with mine own heart; and my' spirit made dili-gent search.
7 Will the LORD cast' off for ever?
 And will' he be favourable no more?
8 Is his mercy clean' gone for ever?
 Doth his promise' fail for e-ver-more?
9 Hath God for'gotten to be‿gracious?
 Hath he in anger shut' up his ten-der mercies? Selah.
10 And I said, This is' my in-firmity:
 But I will remember the years of the' right hand of the‿Most High.
11 I will remember the' works of the‿Lord:
 Surely I will re'member thy wonders of old.
12 I will meditate also of' all thy work,
 And' talk of thy doings.
13 Thy way, O God, is' in the sanctuary:
 Who is so' great a God as our‿God!
14 Thou art the God that' do-est wonders:
 Thou hast declared thy' strength a-mong the people.
15 Thou hast with thine arm re'deemed thy people,
 The' sons of Jacob and Joseph. Selah.
16 The waters saw thee, O God, the' wa-ters saw‿thee;
 They were afraid: the' depths also were troubled.
17 The clouds poured out water: the skies' sent out a‿sound:
 Thine arrows' al-so went a-broad.
18 The voice of thy thunder was' in the heaven:
 The lightnings lightened the world; the' earth trembled and shook.

PSALMS.

19 Thy way is in the sea, and thy path in the' grēat waters,
And thy' foot-steps are not known.
20 Thou leddest thy people' like a flock
By the' hand of Moses and Aaron.

PSALM LXXVIII.
¶ Maschil of Asaph.

GIVE ear, O my people', to my law:
Incline your ears to the' wŏrds of my mouth.
2 I will open my' mouth in a parable:
I will' utter dark sayings of old:
3 Which we have' heard and known,
And' ŏur fathers have told us.
4 We will not hide them from their children,
showing to the generation to come the' praises of the LORD,
And his strength, and his wonderful' works that he hath done.
5 For he established a testimony in Jacob, and appointed a' law in Israel,
Which he commanded our fathers, that they should' make them known to their children:
6 That the generation to come might know them,
even the children which' should be born;
Who should arise and de'clare them to their children;
7 That they might set their' hope in God,
And not forget the works of God, but' kĕep his com-mandments:
8 And might not be as their fathers, a stubborn and re'bellious gene-ration;
A generation that set not their heart aright, and whose spirit' was not steadfast with God.
9 The children of Ephraim, being armed, and' carrying bows,
Turned' back in the day of battle.

PSALMS.

10 They kept not the' covenant of God,
   And refused to' wälk in his law;
11 And for'gat his works,
   And his' wonders that he had showed‿them.
12 Marvellous things did he in the' sight of‿their fathers,
   In the land of Egypt', in the field of Zoan.
13 He divided the sea, and caused them to' päss through;
   And he made the waters to' ständ as an heap.
14 In the daytime also he led them' with a cloud,
   And all the' night with a‿light of fire.
15 He clave the' rocks in the‿wilderness,
   And gave them drink as' out of the‿grëat depths.
16 He brought streams also' out of the‿rock,
   And caused waters to' rün down like rivers.
17 And they sinned yet' more a-gainst‿him,
   By provoking the' Most High in the wilderness.
18 And they tempted God' in their heart,
   By' asking meat for their lust.
19 Yea, they' spake against God;
   They said, Can God furnish a' ta-ble in the wilderness?
20 Behold, he smote the rock, that the waters gushed out, and the' streams over-flowed;
   Can he give bread also? Can he pro'vide flesh for his people?
21 Therefore the LORD heard this', and was wroth:
   So a fire was kindled against Jacob, and anger also' cäme up against Israel;
22 Because they believed' not in God,
   And trusted' not in his sal-vation:
23 Though he had commanded the' clouds from above,
   And' opened the doors of heaven,
24 And had rained down manna upon' them to eat,
   And had' given‿them of the‿corn of heaven.
25 Man did eat' an-gels' food:
   He' sent them meat to the‿full.

PSALMS.

26 He caused an east wind to' blow in the‿heaven:
   And by his power he' brŏught in the south‿wind.
27 He rained flesh also up'on‿them as dust,
   And feathered fowls' like‿as the sand of the‿sea;
28 And he let it fall in the' midst of‿their camp,
   Round a'bout their ha-bi-tations.
29 So they did eat, and' were well filled:
   For he' gave‿them their own de-sire;
30 They were not estranged' from their lust.
   But while their' meat was yet in their‿mouths,
31 The wrath of God' came up-on‿them,
   And slew the fattest of them, and smote down the' cho-sen men of Israel.
32 For all this they' sin-ned still,
   And believed not' for his won-drous works.
33 Therefore their days did he con'sume in vanity,
   A'nd their years in trouble.
34 When he slew them', then they sought‿him:
   And they returned and inquired' ear-ly af-ter God.
35 And they remembered that God' was their rock,
   And the' high God their re-deemer.
36 Nevertheless they did flatter him' with their mouth,
   And they lied un'to him with their tongues.
37 For their heart was' not right with‿him,
   Neither were they' stead-fast in his covenant.
38 But he, being full of compassion, forgave their iniquity, and de'stroyed them not:
   Yea, many a time turned he his anger away, and did not' stir up all his wrath.
39 For he remembered that they' were but flesh;
   A wind that passeth away, and' com-eth not a-gain.
40 How oft did they provoke him' in the wilderness,
   And' grieve him in the desert!
41 Yea, they turned back and' tempt-ed God,
   And limited the' Ho-ly One of Israel.
42 They remembered' not his hand,
   Nor the day when he de'livered them from the enemy.

PSALMS.

43 How he had wrought his' signs in Egypt,
   And his' wonders in the‿field of Zoan:
44 And had turned their' rivers into blood;
   And their floods', that they could not drink.
45 He sent divers sorts of flies among them', which de-voured‿them;
   And' frögs, which de-stroyed‿them.
46 He gave also their increase' unto the caterpillar,
   And their' la-bour unto the locust.
47 He destroyed their' vines with hail,
   And their' syca-more trees with frost.
48 He gave up their cattle also' to the hail,
   And their' flöcks to hot thunderbolts.
49 He cast upon them the fierceness of his anger,
   wrath, and indig'nation, and trouble,
   By sending' e-vil angels a-mong‿them.
50 He made a' way to‿his anger;
   He spared not their soul from death, but gave their' life over to the pestilence.
51 And smote all the' firstborn in Egypt;
   The chief of their strength' in the tabernacles of Ham:
52 But made his own people to go' forth like sheep,
   And guided them in the' wilder-ness like a flock.
53 And he led them on safely', so‿that they feared‿not:
   But the' sea over-whelmed their enemies.
54 And he brought them to the' border of‿his sanc-tuary,
   Even to this mountain, which' his right hand had purchased.
55 He cast out the heathen also before them, and divided them an in'heritance by line,
   And made the tribes of Israel to' dwëll in their tents.
56 Yet they tempted and provoked the' Most High God,
   And' këpt not his testimonies:

PSALMS.

57 But turned back, and dealt unfaithfully' like their fathers:
 They were turned aside' like a de-ceit-ful bow.
58 For they provoked him to anger' with their high places,
 And moved him to jealousy' with their gra-ven images.
59 When God heard this', he was wroth,
 And' greatly ab-hor-red Israel:
60 So that he forsook the' tabernacle of Shiloh,
 The tent' which he placed among men;
61 And delivered his strength' into cap-tivity,
 And his glory' into the ene-my's hand.
62 He gave his people over also' unto the sword;
 And was' wroth with his in-heritance.
63 The fire consumed their' young men;
 And their maidens' were not given to marriage.
64 Their priests' fell by the sword;
 And their widows' made no la-men-tation.
65 Then the LORD awaked as one' out of sleep,
 And like a mighty man that' shouteth by reason of wine.
66 And he smote his enemies in the' hin-der part:
 He put them' to a per-petual re-proach.
67 Moreover he refused the' tabernacle of Joseph,
 And' chose not the tribe of Ephraim:
68 But chose the' tribe of Judah,
 The mount' Zi-on which he loved.
69 And he built his sanctuary' like high palaces,
 Like the earth which he' hath es-tablished for ever.
70 He chose David' also his servant,
 And' took him from the sheepfolds:
71 From following the ewes' great with young,
 He brought him to feed Jacob his people, and Is-rael his in-heritance.
72 So he fed them according to the integrity' of his heart;
 And guided them by the' skilful-ness of his hands.

PSALMS.

PSALM LXXIX.

¶ A Psalm of Asaph.

O GOD, the heathen are come into' thine inheritance:
Thy holy temple have they defiled; they have' laid Je-rusalem on heaps.
2 The dead bodies of thy servants have they given to be meat unto the' fowls of the‿heaven,
The flesh of thy saints' unto the beasts of the‿earth.
3 Their blood have they shed like water round a'bout Je-rusalem;
And' there was none to bury‿them.
4 We are become a re'proach to‿our neighbours,
A scorn and derision to' them that‿are round a-bout‿us.
5 How long, LORD? wilt thou be' angry for ever?
Shall thy' jealous-y burn like fire?
6 Pour out thy wrath upon the heathen that' have not known‿thee,
And upon the kingdoms that have not' called up-on thy name.
7 For they have de'vour-ed Jacob,
And' läid waste his dwelling‿place.
8 O remember not against us former iniquities; let thy tender mercies' speedily pre-vent‿us:
For' we are brought very low.
9 Help us, O God of our salvation, for the' glory of‿thy name:
And deliver us, and purge away our' sins, for thy name's sake.
10 Wherefore should the heathen say', Where‿is their God?
Let him be known among the heathen in our sight, by the revenging of the blood of thy' ser-vants which is shed.

PSALMS.

11 Let the sighing of the prisoner' come be-fore‿thee:
According to the greatness of thy power preserve
thou those that' are ap-pointed to die;
12 And render unto our neighbours sevenfold into
their bosom' their re-proach,
Wherewith they have re'proach-ed thee, O LORD.
13 So we thy people, and sheep of thy pasture, will
give thee' thanks for ever:
We will show forth thy' praise to all gene-rations.

PSALM LXXX.

¶ To the chief Musician upon Shoshannim-eduth, A Psalm
of Asaph.

GIVE ear, O Shepherd of Israel, thou that leadest
Joseph' like a flock;
Thou that dwellest be'tween the cherubims, shine
forth.
2 Before Ephraim, and' Benjamin, and Manasseh,
Stir up thy' strength, and come and save‿us.
3 Turn us again, O God, and cause thy' face to shine;
A'nd we shall be saved.
4 O LORD' God of hosts,
How long wilt thou be angry a'gainst the‿prayer
of thy people?
5 Thou feedest them with the' bread of tears:
And givest them' tears to‿drink in great measure.
6 Thou makest us a strife' unto our neighbours;
And our enemies' laugh a-mong them-selves.
7 Turn us again, O' God of hosts,
And cause thy face to shine'; and we shall be
saved.
8 Thou hast brought a vine' out of Egypt:
Thou hast cast out the' heathen, and plant-ed it.
9 Thou preparedst' room be-fore‿it,
And didst cause it to take deep root', and it filled
the land.

101

PSALMS.

10 The hills were covered with the' sha-dow of‿it,
   And the boughs thereof were' like the good-ly cedars.
11 She sent out her boughs' unto the sea,
   And her' branch-es unto the river.
12 Why hast thou then broken' down her hedges,
   So that all they which' pass by the‿way do pluck‿her?
13 The boar out of the' wood doth waste‿it,
   And the wild beast of the' fïeld doth de-vour‿it.
14 Return, we beseech thee, O' God of hosts:
   Look down from heaven, and be'hold, and visit this vine;
15 And the vineyard which thy' right‿hand hath planted,
   And the branch that thou' madest strong for thy-self.
16 It is burned with fire, it' is cut down:
   They perish at the re'büke of thy countenance.
17 Let thy hand be upon the man' of thy right‿hand,
   Upon the son of man whom thou' madest strong for thy-self.
18 So will not we go' back from thee:
   Quicken us, and we will' call up-on thy name.
19 Turn us again, O LORD' God of hosts,
   Cause thy face to shine'; and we shall be saved.

PSALM LXXXI.

¶ To the chief Musician upon Gittith, A Psalm of Asaph.

SING aloud unto' God our strength:
   Make a joyful noise' unto the God of Jacob.
2 Take a psalm, and bring' hither the timbrel,
   The pleasant' härp with the psaltery.
3 Blow up the trumpet' in the‿new moon,
   In the time appointed', on our sol-emn feast‿day.
4 For this was a' statute for Israel,
   And a' law of the‿God of Jacob.

5 This he ordained in Joseph for a testimony, when
    he went out through the' land of Egypt:
  Where I heard a' language that I under-stood‿not.
6 I removed his shoulder' from the burden:
  His hands were de'liver-ed from the pots.
7 Thou calledst in trouble, and' I de-livered‿thee;
  I answered thee in the secret place of thunder: I
    proved thee' at the waters of Meribah.   Selah.
8 Hear, O my people, and I will testify' un-to thee:
  O Israel, if' thou wilt hearken un-to‿me;
9 There shall no strange' god be in‿thee;
  Neither shalt thou' wor-ship any strange god.
10 I am the LORD thy God, which brought thee out of
    the' land of Egypt:
  Open thy mouth' wide, and I will fill‿it.
11 But my people would not hearken' to my voice;
  And' Israel would none of me.
12 So I gave them up unto their' own hearts' lust:
  And they' walked in their own counsels.
13 Oh that my people had hearkened' un-to me,
  And Israel had' walk-ed in my ways!
14 I should soon have sub'dued their enemies,
  And turned my' hand a-gainst their adversaries.
15 The haters of the LORD should have submitted
    themselves' un-to him:
  But their time' should have endured for ever.
16 He should have fed them also with the' finest of
    the‿wheat:
  And with honey out of the rock should' I have
    satis-fied thee.

PSALM LXXXII.

¶ A Psalm of Asaph.

GOD standeth in the congre'gation of the‿mighty;
He' judgeth a-mong the gods.

PSALMS.

2 How long will ye' judge un-justly,
    And ac'cept the persons of the͜ wicked? Selah.
3 Defend the' poor and fatherless:
    Do justice' to the͜ af-flicted and needy.
4 Deliver the' poor and needy:
    Rid them out of the' hand of the wicked.
5 They know not, neither will they understand;
        they walk' on in darkness:
    All the foundations of the' earth are out of course.
6 I have said', Ye are gods;
    And all of you are' chil-dren of the͜ Most High.
7 But ye shall' die like men,
    And' fall like one of the͜ princes.
8 Arise, O God', judge the earth:
    For' thou shalt inherit all nations.

PSALM LXXXIII.

¶ A Song or Psalm of Asaph.

KEEP not thou' silence, O God;
    Hold not thy peace, and' be not still, O God.
2 For, lo, thine enemies' make a tumult:
    And they that hate thee have' lift-ed up'the head.
3 They have taken crafty counsel' against thy people,
    And con'sulted a-gainst thy hidden͜ ones.
4 They have said, Come, and let us cut them off
        from' being a nation;
    That the name of Israel may be' no more in
        re-membrance.
5 For they have consulted together with' one con-sent:
    They' are con-federate a-gainst͜ thee:
6 The tabernacles of Edom' and the Ishmaelites;
    Of' Mo-ab, and the Hagarenes;
7 Gebal, and' Ammon, and Amalek;
    The Philistines' with the͜ in-habitants of Tyre;
8 Assur also is' join-ed with͜ them:
    They have' holpen the children of Lot. Selah.

PSALMS.

9 Do unto them as' unto the Midianites;
  As to Sisera, as to Jabin', at the brook of Kison:
10 Which' perished at Endor:
  They be'came as dung for the earth.
11 Make their nobles like Oreb' and like Zeeb:
  Yea, all their princes as' Zebah and as Zal-munna:
12 Who said, Let us' take to ourselves
  The' houses of God in possession.
13 O my God, make them' like a wheel;
  As the' stubble be-fore the wind.
14 As the fire' burneth a wood,
  And as the flame' setteth the mountains on fire;
15 So persecute them' with thy tempest,
  And make them a'fräid with thy storm.
16 Fill their' faces with shame;
  That they may' seek thy name, O Lord.
17 Let them be confounded and' troubled for ever;
  Yea, let them be' put to shame and perish:
18 That men may know that thou, whose name' alone is JEHOVAH,
  Art the Most' High over all the earth.

PSALM LXXXIV.

¶ To the chief Musician upon Gittith, A Psalm for the sons of Korah.

HOW amiable' are thy tabernacles,
  O' Lörd of hosts!
2 My soul longeth, yea, even fainteth for the' courts of the Lord:
  My heart and my flesh crieth out' for the liv-ing God.
3 Yea, the sparrow hath found an house, and the swallow a nest for herself, where she may' lay her young,
  Even thine altars, O Lord of hosts, my' King and my God.

PSALMS.

4 Blessed are they that' dwell in‿thy house:
 They will' be still prais-ing thee. Selah.
5 Blessed is the man whose' strength is‿in thee;
 In whose heart' are the ways of them.
6 Who passing through the valley of Baca' make‿it a well;
 The' rain also filleth the pools.
7 They go from' strength to strength,
 Every one of them in Zion ap'peareth be-főre God.
8 O LORD God of hosts', hear my prayer:
 Give' ear, O God of Jacob. Selah.
9 Behold, O' God, our shield,
 And look upon the' face of thine an-ointed.
10 For a day in thy courts is' better than a‿thousand.
 I had rather be a doorkeeper in the house of my God, than to' dwell in the‿tents of wickedness.
11 For the LORD God is a sun and shield: the Lord will give' grace and glory:
 No good thing will he withhold from' them that walk up-rightly.
12 O' LORD of hosts,
 Blessed is the' man that trusteth in thee.

PSALM LXXXV.

¶ To the chief Musician, A Psalm for the sons of Korah.

LORD, thou hast been favourable' unto thy land:
 Thou hast brought' back the‿cap-tivity of Jacob.
2 Thou hast forgiven the iniquity' of thy people,
 Thou hast' cover-ed all their sin. Selah.
3 Thou hast taken away' all thy wrath:
 Thou hast turned thyself from the' fierce-ness of thine anger.
4 Turn us, O God of' our sal-vation,
 And cause thine' anger towards us to cease.
5 Wilt thou be angry with' us for ever?
 Wilt thou draw out thine' anger to all gene-rations?

6 Wilt thou not re′vive us again:
   That thy people′ may re-joice in thee?
7 Show us thy′ mercy, O LORD,
   And′ grant us thy sal-vation.
8 I will hear what God the′ LORD will speak:
   For he will speak peace unto his people, and to his saints: but let them not′ turn a-gain to folly.
9 Surely his salvation is nigh′ them that fear‿him;
   That′ glory may dwell in‿our land.
10 Mercy and truth are′ met to-gether;
    Righteousness and′ peace have kissed each other.
11 Truth shall spring′ out of the‿earth;
    And righteousness′ shall look down from heaven.
12 Yea, the LORD shall give that′ which is good;
    And our′ land shall yield her increase.
13 Righteousness shall′ go be-fore‿him;
    And shall set us′ in the‿way of his steps.

PSALM LXXXVI.

¶ A Prayer of David.

BOW down thine ear′, O LORD, hear‿me:
   For′ I am poor and needy.
2 Preserve my soul; for′ I am holy:
   O thou my God, save thy′ servant that trusteth in thee.
3 Be merciful unto′ me, O LORD:
   For I′ cry un-to thee daily.
4 Rejoice the′ soul of‿thy servant:
   For unto thee, O LORD, do′ I lift up my soul.
5 For thou, LORD, art good, and′ ready to forgive;
   And plenteous in mercy unto all′ them that call up-on‿thee.
6 Give ear, O LORD′, unto my prayer;
   And attend to the′ voice of‿my sup-pli-cations.
7 In the day of my trouble I will′ call up-on‿thee:
   For′ thou wilt an-swer me.

PSALMS.

8 Among the gods there is none like unto' thee,
    O LORD :
  Neither are there any works' like un-to thy works.
9 All nations whom thou hast made shall come and
    worship before' thee, O LORD;
  A'nd shall glorify thy name.
10 For thou art great, and doest' won-drous things:
  Th'ou art God a-lone.
11 Teach me thy way, O LORD ; I will' walk in thy
    truth :
  Unite my' heart to fear thy name.
12 I will praise thee, O LORD my God, with' all my
    heart :
  And I will glorify thy' name for e-ver-more.
13 For great is thy' mer-cy toward me :
  And thou hast delivered my' soul from the low-est
    hell.
14 O God, the proud are risen against me, and the
    assemblies of violent men have sought' after my
    soul ;
  And' have not set thee be-fore them.
15 But thou, O LORD, art a God full of com'passion,
    and gracious;
  Long-suffering, and' plenteous in mercy and truth.
16 O turn unto me, and have' mercy up-on me;
  Give thy strength unto thy servant, and' save the son
    of thine handmaid.
17 Show me a token for good: that they which hate
    me may see it, and' be a-shamed :
  Because thou, LORD, hast' holp-en me, and com-
    forted me.

PSALM LXXXVII.

¶ A Psalm or Song for the sons of Korah.

HIS' föun-dation
  Is' in the ho-ly mountains.

PSALMS.

2 The LORD loveth the' gates of Zion
More than' all the dwellings of Jacob.
3 Glorious things are' spoken of thee,
O' cĭ-ty of God. Selah.
4 I will make mention of Rahab and Babylon to'
them that know‿me:
Behold Philistia, and Tyre, with Ethiopia'; this
man was‿börn there:
5 And of Zion it shall be said, This and that man was'
born in her:
And the' Highest him-self shall establish‿her.
6 The LORD shall count, when he writeth' up the
people,
That' this man was born there. Selah.
7 As well the singers as the players on instruments'
shall be there:
All my' sprĭngs are in thee.

PSALM LXXXVIII.

¶ A Song or Psalm for the sons of Korah; to the chief Musician upon Mahalath Leannoth. Maschil of Heman the Ezrahite.

O LORD God of' my sal-vation,
I have cried' day and night be-fore‿thee:
2 Let my prayer' come be-fore‿thee:
Incline thine' ear un-to my cry;
3 For my soul is' full of troubles:
And my life draweth' nigh un-to the grave.
4 I am counted with them that go down' into the
pit:
I am as a' man that hath no strength:
5 Free among the dead, like the slain that lie in the
grave, whom thou re'memberest no more;
And they are' cut off from thy hand.
6 Thou hast laid me in the' low-est pit,
In' dark-ness, in the deeps.

PSALMS.

7 Thy wrath lieth' hard up-on‿me,
  And thou hast afflicted' me with all thy waves.
  Selah.
8 Thou hast put away mine acquaintance far' from
    me: thou hast made me an abomi'nation
    un-to‿them:
  I am shut up, and' I can not come forth.
9 Mine eye mourneth by' reason of affliction:
  LORD, I have called daily upon thee, I have
    stretched' out my hands un-to‿thee.
10 Wilt thou show wonders' to the dead?
  Shall the' dead a-rise and praise‿thee? Selah.
11 Shall thy lovingkindness be de'clared in the‿grave?
  Or thy' faithful-ness in de-struction?
12 Shall thy wonders be' known in the‿dark?
  And thy righteousness in the' länd of for-getfulness?
13 But unto thee have I' cried, O LORD;
  And in the morning' shall my prayer pre-vent‿thee.
14 LORD, why castest thou' off my soul?
  Why' hidest thou thy face from‿me?
15 I am afflicted and ready to die from my' yöuth up:
  While I suffer thy' terrors, I am dis-tracted.
16 Thy fierce wrath' go-eth over‿me;
  Thy' terrors have cut me off.
17 They came round about me' daily like water;
  They compassed' me a-bout to-gether.
18 Lover and friend hast thou' put far from‿me,
  And mine ac'quaint-ance in-to darkness.

PSALM LXXXIX.

¶ Maschil of Ethan the Ezrahite.

I WILL sing of the mercies of the' LORD for ever:
  With my mouth will I make known thy' faithfulness
    to all gene-rations.

2 For I have said, Mercy shall be built' up for ever:
  Thy faithfulness shalt thou establish' in the ve-ry heavens.
3 I have made a covenant' with my chosen,
  I have sworn' un-to David my servant,
4 Thy seed will I es'tablish for ever,
  And build up thy' throne to all gene-rations. Selah.
5 And the heavens shall praise thy' wonders, O Lord:
  Thy faithfulness also in the congre'ga-tion of the saints.
6 For who in the heaven can be compared' unto the Lord?
  Who among the sons of the mighty can be' likened un-to the Lord?
7 God is greatly to be feared in the as'sembly of the saints,
  And to be had in reverence of all' them that are a-bout him.
8 O Lord God of hosts, who is a strong Lord' like unto thee?
  Or to thy' faithful-ness round a-bout thee?
9 Thou rulest the' raging of the sea:
  When the waves' thereof a-rise, thou stillest them.
10 Thou hast broken Rahab in pieces, as' one that is slain;
  Thou hast scattered thine' enemies with thy strong arm.
11 The heavens are thine, the earth' also is thine:
  As for the world and the fulness thereof', thou hast found-ed them.
12 The north and the south thou' hast cre-ated them:
  Tabor and Hermon shall re'joice in thy name.
13 Thou hast a' might-y arm:
  Strong is thy hand, and' high is thy right hand.
14 Justice and judgment are the habitation' of thy throne:
  Mercy and truth shall' go be-fore thy face.

PSALMS.

15 Blessed is the people that know the' joy-ful sound:
 They shall walk, O LORD, in the' light of thy countenance.
16 In thy name shall they rejoice' all the day:
 And in thy righteousness' shall they be ex-alted.
17 For thou art the' glory of‿their strength:
 And in thy favour our' horn shall be ex-alted.
18 For the LORD is' our de-fence;
 And the Holy One of' Is-rael is our king.
19 Then thou spakest in vision to the' Holy‿One, and saidst,
 I have laid help upon one that is mighty; I have exalted one' chosen out of the people.
20 I have found' David my servant;
 With my holy' oil have I an-ointed‿him:
21 With whom my hand' shall be established:
 Mine' ärm also shall strengthen‿him.
22 The enemy shall not ex'act up-on‿him;
 Nor the' son of wickedness af-flict‿him.
23 And I will beat down his foes be'fore his face,
 And' plägue them that hate‿him.
24 But my faithfulness and my mercy' shall be with‿him:
 And in my name' shall his horn be exalted.
25 I will set his hand also' in the sea,
 And his' right hand in the rivers.
26 He shall cry unto me', Thou art my‿Father,
 My God, and the' Rock of my sal-vation.
27 Also I will' make‿him my firstborn,
 Higher than the' kïngs of the earth.
28 My mercy will I keep for him for' e-ver-more,
 And my' covenant shall stand fast with‿him.
29 His seed also will I make to en'dure for ever,
 And his' throne as the‿days of heaven.
30 If his children for'sake my law,
 And' walk not in my judgments;
31 If they' break my statutes,
 And' keep not my com-mandments;

PSALMS.

32 Then will I visit their transgression' with the rod,
And' their in-iquity with stripes.
33 Nevertheless my lovingkindness will I not' utterly take from‿him,
Nor' suffer my faithfulness to fail.
34 My covenant will' I not break,
Nor alter the thing that is' gone out of my lips.
35 Once have I sworn' by my holiness,
That I' will not lie unto David.
36 His seed shall' endure for ever,
And his throne' as the sun be-fore‿me.
37 It shall be established for' ever as the‿moon,
And as a' faith-ful witness in heaven. Selah.
38 But thou hast cast off' and ab-horred,
Thou hast been' wroth with thine an-ointed.
39 Thou hast made void the covenant' of thy servant:
Thou hast profaned his crown by' casting it to the ground.
40 Thou hast broken down' all his hedges;
Thou hast' brought his strong‿holds to ruin.
41 All that pass by the' wäy spoil‿him:
He is a re'prŏach to his neighbours.
42 Thou hast set up the right hand' of his adversaries:
Thou hast made' all his enemies to rejoice.
43 Thou hast also turned the' edge of his‿sword,
And hast not' made‿him to stand in the‿battle.
44 Thou hast made his' glory to cease,
And cast his' throne down to the ground.
45 The days of his youth' hast thou shortened:
Thou hast' cover-ed him with shame. Selah.
46 How long, LORD? wilt thou hide thy'self for ever?
Shall thy' wräth burn like fire?
47 Remember how short' my time is:
Wherefore hast thou' made all men in vain?
48 What man is he that liveth, and shall' not see death?
Shall he deliver his soul from the' händ of the grave? Selah.

H

PSALMS.

49 LORD, where are thy former' lov-ing-kindnesses,
    Which thou swarest unto' Da-vid in thy truth?
50 Remember, LORD, the reproach' of thy servants;
    How I do bear in my bosom the reproach of' all the might-y people;
51 Wherewith thine enemies have re'proached, O LORD;
    Wherewith they have reproached the' footsteps of thine an-ointed.
52 Blessed be the LORD' for ever-more.
    A'mĕn and A-men.

PSALM XC.

¶ A Prayer of Moses, the man of God.

LORD, thou hast' been our dwelling-place
    In' äll ge-ne-rations.
2 Before the mountains were brought forth, or ever thou hadst formed the' earth and the⌣world,
    Even from everlasting to ever'last-ing, thou art God.
3 Thou turnest' man to destruction;
    And sayest, Re'turn, ye children of men.
4 For a thousand years in thy sight are but as yesterday when' it is past,
    And' as a watch in the⌣night.
5 Thou carriest them away as with a flood; they are' as a sleep:
    In the morning they are like' grass which grow-eth up.
6 In the morning it flourisheth, and' grow-eth up;
    In the evening it' is cut down, and withereth.
7 For we are consumed' by thine anger,
    And by thy' wräth are we troubled.
8 Thou hast set our' iniquities be-fore⌣thee,
    Our secret sins in the' light of thy countenance.

PSALMS.

9 For all our days are passed away' in thy wrath:
We spend our years' as a‿tale that is told.
10 The days of our years are threescore years and ten;
and if by reason of strength they be' four-score years,
Yet is their strength labour and sorrow; for it is soon cut off', and we fly a-way.
11 Who knoweth the' power of‿thine anger?
Even according to thy' fear, so is thy wrath.
12 So teach us to' number our days,
That we may apply our' hëarts un-to wisdom.
13 Return, O' Lord, how long?
And let it re'pent‿thee con-cerning thy servants.
14 O satisfy us early' with thy mercy;
That we may rejoice and be' gläd all our days.
15 Make us glad according to the days wherein thou' hast af-flicted‿us,
And the years where'in we have seen evil.
16 Let thy work appear' unto thy servants,
And thy' glory un-to their children.
17 And let the beauty of the Lord our' God be upon‿us:
And establish thou the work of our hands upon us; yea, the work of our' hands es-tablish thou it.

PSALM XCI.

HE that dwelleth in the secret place' of the‿Most High,
Shall abide under the' sha-dow of the‿Al-mighty.
2 I will say of the Lord, He is my refuge' and my fortress:
My God'; in him will I trust.
3 Surely he shall deliver thee from the' snare' of the‿fowler,
And' from the noi-some pestilence.

PSALMS.

4 He shall cover thee with his feathers, and under his wings' shalt thou trust:
His truth shall' be thy shield and buckler.
5 Thou shalt not be afraid for the' terror by night;
Nor for the' arrow that flieth by day,
6 Nor for the pestilence that' walketh in darkness;
Nor for the de'struction that wasteth at noonday.
7 A thousand shall fall at thy side, and ten thousand at thy right‿hand;
But it' shall not come nigh thee.
8 Only with thine eyes shalt' thou be-hold,
And' see the reward of the‿wicked.
9 Because thou hast made the LORD, which' is my refuge,
Even the Most' High, thy ha-bi-tation,
10 There shall no' evil be-fall‿thee,
Neither shall any' plague come nigh thy dwelling.
11 For he shall give his' angels charge over‿thee,
To' keep‿thee in all thy ways.
12 They shall bear thee up' in their hands,
Lest thou dash thy' foot a-gainst a stone.
13 Thou shalt tread upon the' lion and adder:
The young lion and the dragon' shalt thou trample under feet.
14 Because he hath set his love upon me, therefore will' I de-liver‿him:
I will set him on high, because' he hath known my name.
15 He shall call upon me, and' I will answer‿him:
I will be with him in trouble; I will de'li-ver him, and honour‿him.
16 With long life' will I satisfy‿him,
And' show him my sal-vation.

PSALMS.

PSALM XCII.

¶ A Psalm or Song for the Sabbath-day.

IT is a good thing to give thanks' unto the LORD,
And to sing praises unto thy' näme, O Most High;
2 To show forth thy lovingkindness' in the morning,
And thy' faithful-ness ev-ery night,
3 Upon an instrument of ten strings, and up'on the psaltery;
Upon the' harp with a‿sol-emn sound.
4 For thou, LORD, hast made me glad' through thy work:
I will triumph in the' wörks of thy hands.
5 O LORD, how great' are thy works!
And thy' thoughts are ve-ry deep.
6 A brutish man' know-eth not;
Neither' doth a fool under-stand‿this.
7 When the wicked spring as the grass, and when all the workers of in'iquity do flourish;
It is that they' shall be destroyed for ever:
8 But' thöu, LORD,
Art most' high for ev-er-more.
9 For, lo, thine enemies, O LORD, for, lo, thine' enemies shall perish;
All the workers of in'iqui-ty shall be scattered;
10 But my horn shalt thou exalt like the' horn of an‿unicorn:
I shall be an'oint-ed with fresh oil.
11 Mine eye also shall see my desire' on mine enemies;
And mine ears shall hear my desire of the wicked that' rïse up a-gainst‿me.
12 The righteous shall flourish' like the palm‿tree:
He shall' grow like a‿cedar in Lebanon.
13 Those that be planted in the' house of the‿LORD
Shall flourish in the' cöurts of our God.

PSALMS.

14 They shall still bring forth fruit' in old age
They' shall be fat and flourishing;
15 To show that the' LORD is upright:
He is my rock, and there is' no un-righteousness in him.

PSALM XCIII.

THE LORD reigneth, he is clothed with majesty;
the LORD is clothed with strength, wherewith he hath' girded him-self;
The world also is stablished, that' it can-not be moved.
2 Thy throne is' established of old:
Thou' art from ev-er-lasting.
3 The floods have lifted up, O LORD, the floods have lifted' up their voice;
The' floods lift up their waves.
4 The LORD on high is mightier than the noise of' ma-ny waters,
Yea, than the' might-y waves of the‿sea.
5 Thy testimonies are' ve-ry sure:
Holiness becometh thine' house, O LORD, for ever.

PSALM XCIV.

O LORD God, to whom' vengeance be-longeth;
O God, to whom vengeance be'long-eth, show thy-self.
2 Lift up thyself, thou' judge of the‿earth:
Render a re'wärd to the proud.
3 LORD, how' long shall the‿wicked,
How' long shall the‿wick-ed triumph?
4 How long shall they utter and' speak hard things?
And all the workers of in'iqui-ty boast them-selves?

PSALMS.

5 They break in pieces thy′ people, O LORD,
A′nd af-flict thine heritage.
6 They slay the′ widow and the‿stranger,
A′nd murder the fatherless.
7 Yet they say, The LORD′ shall not see,
Neither shall the′ God of Jacob re-gard‿it.
8 Understand, ye brutish a′mong the people:
And, ye fools′, when will ye be wise?
9 He that planted the ear, shall′ he not hear?
He that formed the′ eye, shall he not see?
10 He that chastiseth the heathen, shall not′ he cor-rect?
He that teacheth man′ knowledge, shall not he know?
11 The LORD knoweth the′ thoughts of man,
Th′ät they are vanity.
12 Blessed is the man whom thou′ chastenest, O LORD,
And′ teachest him out‿of thy law;
13 That thou mayest give him rest from the′ days of adversity,
Until the pit be′ dig-ged for the wicked.
14 For the LORD will not cast′ off his people,
Neither will he for′säke his in-heritance:
15 But judgment shall return′ un-to righteousness:
And all the′ upright in heart shall follow‿it.
16 Who will rise up for me against the′ e-vil-doers?
Or who will stand up for me against the′ work-ers of in-iquity?
17 Unless the LORD had′ been my help,
My soul had′ al-most dwelt in silence.
18 When I said, My′ föot slippeth;
Thy mercy′, O LORD, held me up.
19 In the multitude of my′ thoughts with-in‿me,
Thy′ comforts de-light my soul.
20 Shall the throne of iniquity have′ fellowship with thee,
Which frameth′ mis-chief by a law

PSALMS.

21 They gather themselves together against the' soul
   of the‿righteous,
   And con'demn the inno-cent blood.
22 But the Lord is' my de-fence;
   And my God is the' röck of my refuge.
23 And he shall bring upon them their own iniquity,
   and shall cut them off in their' öwn wickedness;
   Yea, the Lörd our' God shall cut them off.

PSALM XCV.

O COME, let us sing un'to the Lord:
   Let us make a joyful noise to the' Rock of our
   sal-vation.
2 Let us come before his' presence with thanksgiving,
   And make a joyful noise' un-to him with psalms.
3 For the Lord is a' grëat God,
   And a great' King a-bove all gods.
4 In his hand are the deep' places of the‿earth:
   The strength of the' hills is his also.
5 The sea is his', and he made‿it:
   And his hands' form-ed the‿drÿ land.
6 O come, let us worship and' böw down:
   Let us kneel be'fore the Lord our Maker.
7 For he' is our God;
   And we are the people of his pasture, and the'
   shëep of his hand.
8 To-day, if ye will hear his voice, harden' not your
   heart,
   As in the provocation, and as in the day of
   tempt'a-tion in the wilderness:
9 When your' fa-thers tempted‿me,
   Proved' me, and saw my work.
10 Forty years long was I grieved with this gene'ration,
   and said,
   It is a people that do err in their heart, and they'
   have not known my ways:

PSALMS.

11 Unto whom I sware' in my wrath,
That they should not' en-ter into my rest.

PSALM XCVI.

O SING unto the LORD a' nëw song:
Sing unto the' LÖRD, all the earth.
2 Sing unto the LORD', bless his name;
Show forth his sal'vation from day to day.
3 Declare his glory a'mong the heathen,
His' wonders a-mong all people.
4 For the LORD is great, and' greatly to‿be praised:
He is to be' fear-ed above all gods.
5 For all the gods of the' nations are idols:
But the' LÖRD made the heavens.
6 Honour and majesty' are be-fore‿him:
Strength and' beauty are in his sanctuary.
7 Give unto the LORD, O ye' kindreds of the‿people,
Give unto the' LÖRD glory and strength.
8 Give unto the LORD the glory due' unto his name:
Bring an offering', and come into his courts.
9 O worship the LORD in the' beauty of holiness:
Fear be'fore him, all the earth.
10 Say among the heathen that the' LÖRD reigneth:
The world also shall be established that it shall not be moved: he shall' judge the peo-ple righteously.
11 Let the heavens rejoice, and let the' earth be glad;
Let the sea roar', and the fulness there-of.
12 Let the field be joyful, and all that' is there-in:
Then shall all the trees of the wood re'joice be-fore the LORD:
13 For he cometh, for he cometh to' judge the earth:
He shall judge the world with righteousness, and the' peo-ple with his truth.

PSALMS.

PSALM XCVII.

THE LORD reigneth; let the' earth re-joice;
Let the multitude of' isles be glad there-of.
2 Clouds and darkness are' round a-bout͜ him:
Righteousness and judgment are the habi'ta-tion of his throne.
3 A fire' goeth be-fore͜ him,
And burneth up his' ene-mies round a-bout.
4 His lightnings en'lightened the world:
The' ëarth saw, and trembled.
5 The hills melted like wax at the' presence of the͜ LORD,
At the presence of the' LORD of the͜ whöle earth.
6 The heavens de'clare his righteousness,
And all the' peo-ple see his glory.
7 Confounded be all they that serve graven images, that boast them'selves of idols:
Worship' hïm, all ye gods.
8 Zion heard', and was glad;
And the daughters of Judah rejoiced, be'cause of͜ thy judgments, O LORD.
9 For thou, LORD, art high above' all the earth:
Thou art exalted' far a-bove all gods.
10 Ye that love the' LORD, hate evil:
He preserveth the souls of his saints; he delivereth them' out of the͜ hand of the͜ wicked.
11 Light is' sown for the͜ righteous,
And' gladness for the͜ upright in heart.
12 Rejoice in the' LORD, ye righteous;
And give thanks at the re'mem-brance of his holiness.

PSALMS.

PSALM XCVIII.

¶ A Psalm.

O SING unto the Lord a new song; for he hath done' marvel-lous things:
His right hand, and his holy arm, hath' got-ten him the victory.
2 The Lord hath made known' his sal-vation:
His righteousness hath he openly showed' in the sight of the‿heathen.
3 He hath remembered his mercy and his truth toward the' house of Israel:
All the ends of the earth have seen the sal'va-tion of our God.
4 Make a joyful noise unto the Lord', all the earth:
Make a loud noise, and re'joice, and sïng praise.
5 Sing unto the' Lord with the‿harp;
With the harp, and the' vöice of a psalm.
6 With trumpets, and' sound of cornet,
Make a joyful noise be'fore the Lord, the King.
7 Let the sea roar, and the' fulness there-of;
The world, and' they that dwell there-in.
8 Let the floods' clap their hands:
Let the hills be joyful to'gether be-fore the Lord;
9 For he cometh to' judge the earth:
With righteousness shall he judge the world', and the people with equity.

PSALM XCIX.

THE Lord reigneth; let the' peo-ple tremble:
He sitteth between the cherubims'; let the earth be moved.
2 The Lord is' great in Zion;
And he is' high above all the people.

PSALMS.

3 Let them praise thy great and' terri-ble name;
   F'ör it is holy.
4 The king's strength also' lov-eth judgment;
   Thou dost establish equity, thou executest' judgment
      and righteousness in Jacob.
5 Exalt ye the' LORD our God,
   And worship at his' footstool; for he is holy.
6 Moses and Aaron among his priests, and Samuel
      among them that call up'on his name;
   They called upon the' LÖRD, and he answered them.
7 He spake unto them in the' cloud-y pillar;
   They kept his testimonies, and the' ordi-nance that
      he gave them.
8 Thou answeredst them, O' LORD our God:
   Thou wast a God that forgavest them, though thou
      tookest' vengeance of their in-ventions.
9 Exalt the LORD our God, and worship at his' ho-ly
      hill;
   For the' LORD our God is holy.

PSALM C.

¶ A Psalm of Praise.

MAKE a joyful noise' unto the LORD,
   A'''ll ye lands,
2 Serve the' LORD with gladness:
   Come be'fore his presence with singing.
3 Know ye that the LORD' he is God:
   It is he that hath made us, and not we ourselves;
   we are his people, and the' shëep of his pasture.
4 Enter into his gates with thanksgiving, and into
      his' courts with praise:
   Be thankful unto' him, and bless his name.
5 For the' LORD is good;
   His mercy is everlasting; and his truth en'dureth
      to all gene-rations.

PSALMS.

PSALM CI.

¶ A Psalm of David.

I WILL sing of' mercy and judgment:
Unto thee', O LORD, will I sing.
2 I will behave myself wisely in a perfect way. O,
when wilt thou' come un-to me?
I will walk within my house' with a per-fect heart.
3 I will set no wicked thing be'fore mine eyes:
I hate the work of them that turn aside; it' shall not cleave to me.
4 A froward heart shall' depart from me:
I will not' know a wick-ed person.
5 Whoso privily slandereth his neighbour, him will' I cut off:
Him that hath an high look and a proud' heart will not I suffer.
6 Mine eyes shall be upon the faithful of the land, that they may' dwell with me:
He that walketh in a' perfect way, he shall serve me.
7 He that worketh deceit shall not dwell with'in my house:
He that telleth lies shall' not tarry in my sight.
8 I will early destroy all the' wicked of the land;
That I may cut off all wicked doers' from the city of the LORD.

PSALM CII.

¶ A Prayer of the afflicted, when he is overwhelmed, and poureth out his complaint before the LORD.

HEAR my' prayer, O LORD,
And let my' cry come un-to thee.

PSALMS.

2 Hide not thy face from me in the day when'
   I am in trouble;
   Incline thine ear unto me: in the day when I' call,
   answer me speedily.
3 For my days are con'sumed like smoke,
   And my bones are' burn-ed as an hearth.
4 My heart is smitten, and' withered like grass;
   So that I for'get to eat my bread.
5 By reason of the' voice of my groaning,
   My' bones cleave to my skin.
6 I am like a' pelican of the wilderness:
   I am' like an owl of the desert.
7 I watch, and' am as a sparrow
   A'lone up-on the house top.
8 Mine enemies reproach me' all the day;
   And they that are mad against' me are sworn
   a-gainst me.
9 For I have eaten' ashes like bread,
   And' mingled my drink with weeping,
10 Because of thine indignation' and thy wrath:
   For thou hast lifted me' up, and cast me down.
11 My days are like a shadow' that de-clineth;
   And' I am withered like grass.
12 But thou, O LORD, shalt en'dure for ever;
   And thy remembrance' un-to all gene-rations.
13 Thou shalt arise, and have' mercy upon Zion:
   For the time to favour her', yea, the set time, is come.
14 For thy servants take pleasure' in her stones,
   And' favour the dust there-of.
15 So the heathen shall fear the' name of the LORD,
   And all the' kings of the earth thy glory.
16 When the LORD shall' build up Zion,
   He shall ap'pear in his glory.
17 He will regard the' prayer of the destitute,
   And' not de-spise their prayer.
18 This shall be written for the gene'ration to come:
   And the people which shall be cre'ated shall praise
   the LORD.

PSALMS.

19 For he hath looked down from the' height of‿his
  sanctuary;
  From heaven did the' Lord be-hold the earth;
20 To hear the groaning' of the prisoner;
  To loose those that' are ap-pointed to death;
21 To declare the name of the' Lord in Zion,
  And his' präise in Je-rusalem;
22 When the people are' gathered to-gether,
  And the' kingdoms, to serve the Lord.
23 He weakened my' strength in the‿way;
  He' short-en-ed my days.
24 I said, O my God, take me not away in the' midst
  of my‿days:
  Thy years are' through-out all gene-rations.
25 Of old hast thou laid the foun'dation of the‿earth:
  And the heavens are the' wörk of thy hands.
26 They shall perish, but' thou shalt endure:
  Yea, all of them shall wax old like a garment; as
  a vesture shalt thou change them', and they
  shall be changed:
27 But' thou art the‿same,
  And thy' years shall have no end.
28 The children of thy servants' shall con-tinue,
  And their seed shall' be es-tablished be-fore‿thee.

PSALM CIII.

¶ A Psalm of David.

BLESS the Lord', O my soul:
  And all that is within me', bless his ho-ly name.
2 Bless the Lord', O my soul,
  And for'get not all his benefits:
3 Who forgiveth' all thine iniquities;
  Who' healeth all thy dis-eases;
4 Who redeemeth thy' life from destruction;
  Who crowneth thee with loving'kindness and
  ten-der mercies;

PSALMS.

5 Who satisfieth thy' mouth with good‿things;
  So that thy youth is re'new-ed like the eagle's.
6 The LORD executeth' righteousness and judgment
  For' all that are op-pressed.
7 He made known his' ways unto Moses,
  His acts' unto the children of Israel.
8 The LORD is' merciful and gracious,
  Slow to' anger, and plenteous in mercy.
9 He will not' al-ways chide:
  Neither will he' keep his anger for ever.
10 He hath not dealt with us' after our sins:
  Nor rewarded us ac'cording to our in-iquities.
11 For as the heaven is high' above the earth,
  So great is his' mercy toward them that fear‿him.
12 As far as the east is' from the west,
  So far hath he removed' our trans-gres-sions from‿us.
13 Like as a father' pitieth his children,
  So the LORD' piti-eth them that fear‿him.
14 For he' knoweth our frame:
  He re'membereth that we are dust.
15 As for man, his' days are as‿grass:
  As a flower of the' field, so he flourisheth.
16 For the wind passeth over it, and' it is gone;
  And the place there'of shall know‿it no more.
17 But the mercy of the LORD is from everlasting to everlasting upon' them that fear‿him,
  And his righteousness' un-to child-ren's children;
18 To such as' keep his covenant,
  And to those that remember' his com-mandments to do‿them.
19 The LORD hath prepared his' throne in the‿heavens;
  And his kingdom' rul-eth o-ver all.
20 Bless the LORD, ye his angels, that excel in strength, that' do his commandments,
  Hearkening unto the' vöice of his word.
21 Bless ye the LORD, all' ye his hosts;
  Ye ministers of' his, that do his pleasure.

PSALMS.

22 Bless the LORD, all his works, in all places of′ his do-minion:
Bless the′ LORD, O my soul.

PSALM CIV.

BLESS the LORD′, O my soul,
O LORD my God, thou art very great; thou art′ clothed with honour and majesty.
2 Who coverest thyself with light′ as with a_garment:
Who stretchest′ out the heavens like a_curtain:
3 Who layeth the beams of his chambers′ in the waters:
Who maketh the clouds his chariot: who walketh up′on the wings of the_wind:
4 Who maketh his′ an-gels spirits;
His′ ministers a flam-ing fire:
5 Who laid the foun′dations of the_earth,
That it should′ not be removed for ever.
6 Thou coveredst it with the deep′ as with a_garment:
The waters′ stood a-bove the mountains.
7 At thy re′buke they fled;
At the voice of thy′ thunder they hasted a-way.
8 They go′ up by the_mountains;
They go down by the valleys unto the place which′ thou hast found-ed for_them.
9 Thou hast set a bound that they′ may_not pass over,
That they turn not a′gain to cover the earth.
10 He sendeth the springs′ into the valleys,
Which′ run a-mong the hills.
11 They give drink to every′ beast of the_field:
The wild′ ass-es quench their thirst.
12 By them shall the fowls of the heaven have their′ ha-bi-tation,
Which′ sing a-mong the branches.

I

PSALMS.

13 He watereth the hills' from his chambers:
   The earth is satisfied with the' früit of thy works.
14 He causeth the grass to grow for the cattle, and herb
   for the' service of man,
   That he may bring forth' food out of the earth;
15 And wine that maketh glad the heart of man, and
   oil to make his' face to shine,
   And' bread which strengtheneth man's heart.
16 The trees of the LORD are' full of sap;
   The cedars of' Lebanon, which he hath planted;
17 Where the birds' make their nests:
   As for the stork, the' fir trees are her house.
18 The high hills are a refuge' for the wild goats;
   And the' röcks for the conies.
19 He appointed the' moon for seasons:
   The sun' knoweth his go-ing down.
20 Thou makest darkness, and' it is night:
   Wherein all the beasts of the' fo-rest do creep forth.
21 The young lions roar' after their prey,
   And' seek their meat from God.
22 The sun ariseth, they gather them'selves to-gether,
   And' lay them down in their dens.
23 Man goeth forth' unto his work,
   And to his' labour un-til the evening.
24 O LORD, how manifold' are thy works!
   In wisdom hast thou made them all: the earth is'
   füll of thy riches.
25 So is this great' and wide sea,
   Wherein are things creeping innumerable, both'
   small and grëat beasts.
26 There' go the ships:
   There is that leviathan, whom thou hast' made to
   play there-in.
27 These wait' all upon thee;
   That thou mayest give them their' mëat in due
   season.
28 That thou' givest them they gather:
   Thou openest thine hand', they are filled with good.

29 Thou hidest thy face', they are troubled:
   Thou takest away their breath, they die, and re'türn to their dust.
30 Thou sendest forth thy spirit, they' are cre-ated:
   And thou re'newest the face of the earth.
31 The glory of the LORD shall en'dure for ever:
   The LORD shall re'jöice in his works.
32 He looketh on the earth', and it trembleth:
   He toucheth the' hills, and they smoke.
33 I will sing unto the LORD as' long as I live:
   I will sing praise to my God' while I have my being.
34 My meditation of him' shall be sweet:
   I will be' gläd in the LORD.
35 Let the sinners be consumed out of the earth, and let the wicked' be no more.
   Bless thou the LORD, O my soul'. Präise ye the LORD.

PSALM CV.

O GIVE thanks unto the LORD; call up'on his name:
   Make known his' deeds a-mong the people.
2 Sing unto him, sing' psalms unto him:
   Talk ye of' all his won-drous works.
3 Glory ye in his' ho-ly name:
   Let the heart of them re'joice that seek the LORD.
4 Seek the LORD', and his strength:
   Seek' his face ev-er-more.
5 Remember his marvellous works that' he hath done;
   His wonders, and the' judg-ments of his mouth;
6 O ye seed of' Abraham his servant,
   Ye' children of Jacob his chosen.
7 He is the' LORD our God:
   His judgments' are in all the earth.
8 He hath remembered his' covenant for ever,
   The word which he com'manded to a thousand gene-rations.

PSALMS.

9 Which covenant he' made with Abraham,
And his' öath un-to Isaac;
10 And confirmed the same unto Jacob' for a law,
And to Israel for an' ev-er-last-ing covenant:
11 Saying, Unto thee will I give the' land of Canaan,
The' lot of your in-heritance:
12 When there were but a' few men in number;
Yea, very' few, and stran-gers in it.
13 When they went from one nation' to an-other,
From one' kingdom to anoth-er people,
14 He suffered no man to' do them wrong;
Yea, he re'proved kings for their sakes;
15 Saying, Touch not' mine an-ointed,
And' do my prophets no harm.
16 Moreover, he called for a famine up'on the land:
He' brake the whole staff of bread.
17 He sent a' man be-fore them,
Even Joseph', who was sold for a servant;
18 Whose feet they' hurt with fetters:
He' was laid in iron;
19 Until the time that his' wörd came;
The' word of the Lörd tried him.
20 The king' sent and loosed him;
Even the ruler of the people', and let him go free.
21 He made him' lord of his house,
And' ruler of all his substance:
22 To bind his princes' at his pleasure;
And' teach his sena-tors wisdom.
23 Israel also came' in-to Egypt;
And Jacob sojourned' in the land of Ham.
24 And he increased his' peo-ple greatly,
And made them' strong-er than their enemies.
25 He turned their heart to' hate his people,
To deal' subtile-ly with his servants.
26 He sent' Moses his servant,
And' Aaron whom he had chosen.
27 They showed his' signs a-mong them,
And' wonders in the land of Ham.

PSALMS.

28 He sent darkness, and' made it dark;
   And they re'belled not against his word.
29 He turned their waters' in-to blood,
   And' slĕw their fish.
30 Their land brought forth' frogs in abundance,
   In the' cham-bers of their kings.
31 He spake, and there came divers' sorts of flies,
   And' lice in all their coasts.
32 He gave them' hail for rain,
   And' flaming fire in their land.
33 He smote their vines also', and their fig‿trees;
   And' brake the trees of‿their coasts.
34 He spake, and the' lo-custs came,
   And caterpillars', and that with-out number,
35 And did eat up all the herbs' in their land,
   And devoured the' früit of their ground.
36 He smote also all the firstborn' in their land,
   The' chief of all their strength.
37 He brought them forth also with' silver and gold;
   And there was not one feeble' person a-mong their tribes.
38 Egypt was glad when' they de-parted;
   For the' fear of‿them fell up-on‿them.
39 He spread a' cloud for a‿covering;
   And fire to' give light in the night.
40 The people asked, and he' bröught quails,
   And satisfied them' with the bread of heaven.
41 He opened the rock, and the' waters gushed out;
   They ran in the' dry places like a river.
42 For he remembered his' ho-ly promise,
   A'nd Abraham his servant.
43 And he brought forth his' people with joy,
   A'nd his chosen with gladness;
44 And gave them the' lands of the‿heathen;
   And they inherited the' la-bour of the people;
45 That they might observe his statutes, and' keep his laws.
   Pr'äise ye the LORD.

PSALMS.

PSALM CVI.

PRAISE ye the Lord. O give thanks un'to the Lord;
For he is good: for his' mercy en-dureth for ever.
2 Who can utter the mighty' acts of the‿Lord?
Who can' show forth all his praise?
3 Blessed are they that' kēep judgment,
And he that doeth' righteousness at äll times.
4 Remember me, O Lord, with the favour that thou bearest' unto thy people:
O' visit‿me with thy sal-vation;
5 That I may see the' good of‿thy chosen,
That I may rejoice in the gladness of thy nation,
that I may' glory with thine in-heritance.
6 We have sinned' with our fathers,
We have committed in'iquity, we have done wickedly.
7 Our fathers understood not thy' wonders in Egypt;
They remembered not the multitude of thy mercies;
but provoked him at the sea', even at the‿Rëd Sea.
8 Nevertheless, he saved them for' his name's sake,
That he might make his' mighty power to be known.
9 He rebuked the Red Sea also, and it was' dri-ed up;
So he led them through the' depths, as through the wilderness.
10 And he saved them from the hand of' him that hated‿them,
And redeemed them' from the hand of the‿enemy.
11 And the waters' covered their enemies;
There' was not one of‿them left.
12 Then believed' they his words;
They' sä'ng his praise.
13 They soon for'gat his works;
They' waited not for his counsel:

PSALMS.

14 But lusted exceedingly' in the wilderness,
And' tempted God in the desert.
15 And he gave them' their re-quest;
But sent' lean-ness into their soul.
16 They envied Moses also' in the camp,
And' Aaron the saint of the⌣Lord.
17 The earth opened and' swallowed up Dathan,
And' covered the company of Abiram.
18 And a fire was kindled' in their company;
The flame' burn-ed up the wicked.
19 They made a' calf in Horeb,
And' worshipped the molt-en image.
20 Thus they' changed their glory
Into the similitude of an' ox that eat-eth grass.
21 They forgat' God their Saviour,
Which had' done great things in Egypt;
22 Wondrous works in the' land of Ham,
And' terrible things by the⌣Red Sea.
23 Therefore he said that he would destroy them, had not Moses his chosen stood before him' in the breach,
To turn away his wrath', lest he should de-stroy⌣them.
24 Yea, they despised the' plea-sant land,
They be'liev-ed not his word:
25 But murmured' in their tents,
And hearkened not' unto the voice of the⌣Lord:
26 Therefore he lifted up his' hand a-gainst⌣them,
To over'throw them in the wilderness:
27 To overthrow their seed also a'mong the nations,
And to' scatter them in the lands.
28 They joined themselves also' unto Baal-peor,
And' ate the sacrifices of the⌣dead.
29 Thus they provoked him to anger with' their in-ventions:
And the' plague brake in up-on⌣them.
30 Then stood up Phinehas, and' exe-cuted judgment;
And' so the plague was stayed.

PSALMS.

31 And that was counted unto' him for righteousness.
  Unto all gene'rations for ev-er-more.
32 They angered him also at the' waters of strife,
  So that it went ill with' Mo-ses for their sakes:
33 Because they pro'voked his spirit,
  So that he spake unad'vised-ly with his lips.
34 They did not de'stroy the nations,
  Concerning' whom the LORD com-manded them:
35 But were mingled a'mong the heathen,
  And' lëarn-ed their works.
36 And they' served their idols:
  Which' were a snare un-to them.
37 Yea, they' sacrificed their sons
  And their' daugh-ters un-to devils,
38 And shed innocent blood, even the blood of their
    sons and' of their daughters,
  Whom they sacrificed unto the idols of Canaan;
    and the' land was polluted with blood.
39 Thus were they defiled with' their own works,
  And went a whoring' with their own in-ventions.
40 Therefore was the wrath of the LORD kindled
    a'gainst his people,
  Insomuch that he ab'horred his own in-heritance.
41 And he gave them into the' hand of the heathen;
  And they that' hated them rul-ed over them.
42 Their enemies' also op-pressed them,
  And they were brought into sub'jec-tion under
    their hand.
43 Many times did' he de-liver them;
  But they provoked him with their counsel, and
    were brought' low for their in-iquity.
44 Nevertheless, he regarded' their af-fliction,
  When' hë heard their cry:
45 And he remembered for' them his covenant,
  And repented according to the' multi-tude of his
    mercies.
46 He made them also' to be pitied
  Of all' those that carried them captives.

136

47 Save us, O Lord our God, and gather us from a′mong the heathen,
To give thanks unto thy holy name, and to′ tri-umph in thy praise.
48 Blessed be the Lord God of Israel from everlasting to′ ev-er-lasting:
And let all the people say, A′men. Praise ye the Lord.

PSALM CVII.

O GIVE thanks unto the Lord, for′ he is good:
For his′ mercy en-dureth for ever.
2 Let the redeemed of the′ Lord say so,
Whom he hath redeemed′ from the hand of the‿enemy;
3 And gathered them′ out of the‿lands,
From the east, and from the west, from the′ north, and from the south.
4 They wandered in the wilderness in a′ soli-tary way;
They′ found no city to dwell‿in.
5 Hun′gry and thirsty,
Their′ söul faint-ed in them.
6 Then they cried unto the Lord′ in their trouble,
And he delivered them′ out of their dis-tresses.
7 And he led them forth′ by the‿right way,
That they might go to a′ city of ha-bi-tation.
8 Oh that men would praise the′ Lord for‿his goodness,
And for his wonderful works′ to the children of men!
9 For he satisfieth the′ long-ing soul,
And filleth the′ hun-gry soul with goodness.
10 Such as sit in darkness and in the′ shadow of death,
Being′ bound in affliction and iron:

PSALMS.

11 Because they rebelled against the' words of God,
And contemned the' coun-sel of the‿Most High:
12 Therefore he brought down their' heart with labour;
They fell down, and' there was none to help.
13 Then they cried unto the LORD' in their trouble,
And he saved them' out of their dis-tresses.
14 He brought them out of darkness and the' shadow of death,
And' brake their bands in sunder.
15 Oh that men would praise the' LORD for‿his goodness,
And for his wonderful works' to the children of men!
16 For he hath broken the' gates of brass,
And cut the' bars of iron in sunder.
17 Fools, because of' their trans-gression,
And because of their in'iqui-ties, are af-flicted:
18 Their soul abhorreth all' manner of meat;
And they draw near' unto the gates of death.
19 Then they cry unto the LORD' in their trouble,
And he saveth them' out of their dis-tresses.
20 He sent his' word, and healed‿them,
And de'livered them from their destructions.
21 Oh that men would praise the' LORD for‿his goodness,
And for his wonderful works' to the children of men!
22 And let them sacrifice the' sacrifices of thanksgiving,
And de'clare his works with rejoicing.
23 They that go down to the' sea in ships,
That do' business in grëat waters;
24 These see the' works of the‿LORD,
And his' won-ders in the deep.
25 For he commandeth, and raiseth the' storm-y wind,
Which lifteth' up the waves there-of.
26 They mount up to the heaven, they go down a'gain to the‿depths:
Their soul is' melted be-cause of trouble.

PSALMS.

27 They reel to and fro, and stagger like a' drunk-en man,
And' are at their wit's end.
28 Then they cry unto the LORD' in their trouble,
And he bringeth them' out of their dis-tresses.
29 He maketh the' storm a calm,
So that the' waves there-of are still.
30 Then are they glad because' they be quiet;
So he bringeth them unto' their de-sir-ed haven.
31 Oh that men would praise the' LORD for his goodness,
And for his wonderful works' to the children of men!
32 Let them exalt him also in the congre'gation of the people,
And praise him in the as'sem-bly of the elders.
33 He turneth rivers' into a wilderness,
And the' water-springs into dry ground;
34 A fruitful land' in-to barrenness,
For the wickedness of' them that dwell there-in.
35 He turneth the wilderness into a' stand-ing water,
And' dry ground in-to watersprings.
36 And there he maketh the' hungry to dwell,
That they may prepare a' city for ha-bi-tation;
37 And sow the fields, and' plänt vineyards,
Which' may yield fruits of increase.
38 He blesseth them also, so that they are' multi-plied greatly,
And suffereth not their' cat-tle to de-crease.
39 Again, they are minished, and' brŏught low
Through op'pression, af-fliction, and sorrow.
40 He poureth con'tempt upon princes,
And causeth them to wander in the wilderness', where there is no way.
41 Yet setteth he the poor on high' from af-fliction,
And maketh him' fami-lies like a flock.
42 The righteous shall see it', and re-joice;
And all in'iquity shall stop her mouth.
43 Whoso is wise, and will ob'serve these things,
Even they shall understand the loving kind-ness of the LORD.

PSALMS.

PSALM CVIII.

¶ A Song or Psalm of David.

O GOD, my' heart is fixed;
  I will sing and give' praise, even with my glory.
2 Awake', psaltery and harp:
  I my'self will awäke early.
3 I will praise thee, O LORD, a'mong the people:
  And I will sing praises unto' thee a-mong the nations.
4 For thy mercy is great a'bove the heavens,
  And thy truth' reacheth un-to the clouds.
5 Be thou exalted, O God, a'bove the heavens;
  And thy glory a'böve all the earth;
6 That thy beloved may' be de-livered:
  Save with' thy right hand, and answer me.
7 God hath spoken' in his holiness;
  I will rejoice, I will divide Shechem, and mete' out the valley of Succoth.
8 Gilead is mine; Ma'nasseh is mine;
  Ephraim also is the strength of mine head'; Ju-dah is my lawgiver;
9 Moab is my washpot; over Edom will I cast' out my shoe;
  Over Phi'lis-tia will I triumph.
10 Who will bring me into the' ströng city?
   Who will' lead me in-to Edom?
11 Wilt not thou, O God, who hast' cast us off?
   And wilt not thou, O God', go forth with our hosts?
12 Give us' help from trouble:
   For' vain is the help of man.
13 Through God we' shall do valiantly:
   For he it is that' shall tread down our enemies.

PSALM CIX.

¶ To the chief Musician, A Psalm of David.

HOLD' not thy peace,
    O' Göd of my praise;
2 For the mouth of the wicked, and the mouth of the deceitful are' opened a-gainst me:
They have spoken against me' with a ly-ing tongue.
3 They compassed me about also with' words of hatred;
And fought a'gainst me without a cause.
4 For my love they' are my adversaries:
But I' give myself un-to prayer.
5 And they have rewarded me' evil for good,
And' ha-tred for my love.
6 Set thou a' wicked man over him:
And let Satan' stand at his right hand.
7 When he shall be judged, let him' be con-demned;
And' let his prayer become sin.
8 Let his' days be few;
And let an'oth-er take his office.
9 Let his' children be fatherless,
A'nd his wife a widow.
10 Let his children be continually' vagabonds, and beg:
Let them seek their bread also' out of their desolate places.
11 Let the extortioner catch' all that he hath;
And let the' stran-gers spoil his labour.
12 Let there be none to extend' mercy un-to him:
Neither let there be any to' favour his father-less children.
13 Let his posterity be' cüt off;
And in the generation following let their' name be blot-ted out.
14 Let the iniquity of his fathers be re'membered with the LORD;
And let not the sin of his' mother be blot-ted out.

PSALMS.

15 Let them be before the' LORD con-tinually,
   That he may cut off the memory' of them from the earth.
16 Because that he remembered not to' shöw mercy,
   But persecuted the poor and needy man, that he might even' slay the broken in heart.
17 As he loved cursing, so let it' come un-to‿him:
   As he delighted not in blessing, so' let it be far from‿him.
18 As he clothed himself with cursing like as' with his garment,
   So let it come into his bowels like water, and like' oil in-to his bones.
19 Let it be unto him as the' garment which covereth‿him,
   And for a girdle wherewith' he is girded con-tinually.
20 Let this be the reward of mine adversaries' from the LORD,
   And of them that speak' evil a-gainst my soul.
21 But do thou for me, O GOD the Lord, for' thy name's sake:
   Because thy mercy is' good, de-liver thou me.
22 For I am' poor and needy,
   And my' heart is wounded with-in‿me.
23 I am gone like the shadow when' it de-clineth:
   I am tossed' up and down as the‿locust.
24 My knees are' weak through fasting,
   And my' flësh faileth of fatness.
25 I became also a re'proach un-to‿them:
   When they looked up'on‿me they shaked their heads.
26 Help me, O' LORD my God:
   O save me ac'cord-ing to thy mercy:
27 That they may know that this' is thy hand;
   That' thöu, LORD, hast done‿it.
28 Let them curse', but bless thou:
   When they arise, let them be ashamed; but' let thy servant re-joice.

PSALMS.

29 Let mine adversaries be' clothed with shame,
And let them cover themselves with their own con'fusion, as with a mantle.
30 I will greatly praise the LORD' with my mouth;
Yea, I will' praise him among the multitude.
31 For he shall stand at the right hand' of the poor,
To save him from' those that condemn his soul.

PSALM CX.

¶ A Psalm of David.

THE LORD said un'to my Lord,
Sit thou at my right hand, until I' make thine enemies thy footstool.
2 The LORD shall send the rod of thy strength' out of Zion:
Rule thou' in the midst of thine enemies.
3 Thy people shall be willing in the' day of thy power,
In the beauties of holiness from the womb of the morning: thou' hast the dew of thy youth.
4 The LORD hath sworn, and' will not repent,
Thou art a priest for ever after the' or-der of Mel-chizedek.
5 The LORD' at thy right hand
Shall strike through kings in the' däy of his wrath.
6 He shall judge among the heathen, he shall fill the places' with the dead bodies;
He shall wound the' heads over ma-ny countries.
7 He shall drink of the' brook in the way:
Therefore shall' he lift up the head.

PSALM CXI.

PRAISE ye the LORD. I will praise the LORD with my' whöle heart,
In the assembly of the upright, and' in the con-gre-gation.

PSALMS.

2 The works of the' Lord are great,
  Sought out of all' them␣that have pleasure there-in.
3 His work is' honourable and glorious,
  And his' righteousness en-dureth for ever.
4 He hath made his wonderful works to' be re-membered:
  The Lord is gracious, and' full of com-passion.
5 He hath given meat unto' them that fear␣him:
  He will ever be' mind-ful of his covenant.
6 He hath showed his people the' power of␣his works,
  That he may give them the' heri-tage of the heathen.
7 The works of his hands are' verity and judgment;
  All' his com-mandments are sure.
8 They stand fast for' ever and ever,
  And are' done in truth and uprightness.
9 He sent redemption unto his people: he hath commanded his' covenant for ever:
  Holy and' reve-rend is his name.
10 The fear of the Lord is the be'ginning of wisdom:
  A good understanding have they that do his commandments: his' praise en-dureth for ever.

PSALM CXII.

PRAISE ye the Lord. Blessed is the man that' feareth the Lord,
  That delighteth' greatly in his com-mandments.
2 His seed shall be' mighty upon earth:
  The generation of the' up-right shall be blessed.
3 Wealth and riches shall be' in his house:
  And his' righteousness en-dureth for ever.
4 Unto the upright there ariseth' light in the␣darkness
  He is gracious, and' full of compassion, and righteous.

PSALMS.

5 A good man showeth' favour, and lendeth:
He will guide his af'fairs with dis-cretion.
6 Surely he shall not be' moved for ever:
The righteous shall be in' ev-er-lasting re-membrance.
7 He shall not be afraid of' e-vil tidings:
His heart is fixed', trust-ing in the LORD.
8 His heart is established, he shall' not be afraid,
Until he see his de'sire up-on his enemies.
9 He hath dispersed, he hath' given to the poor;
His righteousness endureth for ever; his horn shall
be exalted with honour.
10 The wicked shall see it, and be grieved; he shall
gnash with his teeth, and' melt a-way:
The de'sire of the wicked shall perish.

PSALM CXIII.

PRAISE' ye the LORD.
Praise, O ye servants of the LORD', praise the name of the LORD.
2 Blessed be the' name of the LORD,
From this time forth' and for ev-er-more.
3 From the rising of the sun, unto the going' down of the same,
The LORD'S' name is to be praised.
4 The LORD is high a'bove all nations,
And his' glory a-bove the heavens.
5 Who is like unto the' LORD our God,
Who' dwell-eth on high;
6 Who' humbleth him-self
To behold the things that are in' heaven, and in the earth!
7 He raiseth up the poor' out of the dust,
And lifteth the' needy out of the dunghill;
8 That he may set' him with princes,
Even with the' prin-ces of his people.

PSALMS.

9 He maketh the barren woman to keep house, and
   to be a joyful' mother of children.
   Pr'äise ye the LORD.

PSALM CXIV.

WHEN Israel went' out of Egypt,
   The house of Jacob from a' people of strängè
     language,
2 Judah' was his sanctuary,
   And' Is-rael his do-minion.
3 The sea' saw‿it, and fled:
   Jor'dan was driv-en back.
4 The mountains' skipped like rams,
   And the' lit-tle hills like lambs.
5 What ailed thee, O thou sea', that thou fleddest?
   Thou Jordan, that' thou wast driv-en back?
6 Ye mountains, that ye' skipped like rams,
   And ye' lit-tle hills, like lambs?
7 Tremble, thou earth, at the' presence of the‿LORD,
   At the' presence of the‿God of Jacob;
8 Which turned the rock into a' stand-ing water,
   The flint' into a fountain of waters.

PSALM CXV.

NOT unto us, O LORD, not unto us, but unto thy'
   name give glory,
   For thy mercy', and for thy truth's sake.
2 Wherefore should the' hea-then say,
   Wh'ere is now their God?
3 But our God is' in the heavens;
   He hath done whatso'ev-er he hath pleased.
4 Their idols are' silver and gold,
   The' work of mën's hands.
5 They have mouths', but they speak‿not;
   Eyes' have they, but they see‿not;

PSALMS.

6 They have ears', but they hear‿not;
  Noses' have they, but they smell‿not;
7 They have hands', but they handle‿not;
  Feet have they, but they walk not: neither' speak
    they through their throat.
8 They that make them are' like un-to‿them;
  So is every' one that trust-eth in‿them.
9 O Israel,' trust‿thou in the‿Lord;
  He is their' hëlp and their shield.
10 O house of Aaron', trust in the‿Lord;
   He is their' hëlp and their shield.
11 Ye that fear the Lord', trust in the‿Lord:
   He is their' hëlp and their shield.
12 The Lord hath been mindful of us'; he will
     bless‿us:
   He will bless the house of Israel, he will' bless
     the house of Aaron.
13 He will bless them that' fear the Lord,
   B'öth small and great.
14 The Lord shall increase you' more and more,
   Y'öu and your children.
15 Ye are' blessed of the‿Lord,
   Which' mäde heaven and earth.
16 The heaven, even the heavens', are the Lord's:
   But the earth hath he given' to the children
     men.
17 The dead' praise‿not the Lord,
   Neither any that' go down in-to silence.
18 But we will bless the Lord from this time forth
     and for' ever-more.
   Pr'ä'ise the Lord.

PSALM CXVI.

I' LOVE the Lord,
  Because he hath heard my voice' and my sup-
    pli-cations.

147

PSALMS.

2 Because he hath inclined his' ear un-to͜ me,
Therefore will I call upon him as' löng as I live.
3 The sorrows of death compassed me, and the pains of hell gat' hold up-on͜ me:
I' förnd trouble and sorrow.
4 Then called I upon the' name of the͜ LORD;
O LORD, I' beseech͜ thee, de-liver my soul.
5 Gracious is the' LORD, and righteous;
Yea', oür God is merciful.
6 The LORD pre'serveth the simple:
I was' brought low, and he helped͜ me.
7 Return unto thy rest', O my soul;
For the LORD' hath dealt bounti-fully with͜ thee.
8 For thou hast delivered my' soul from death,
Mine eyes from tears', and my feet from fall-ing.
9 I will walk be'fore the LORD
In the' länd of the living.
10 I believed, therefore' have I spoken:
I' wäs greatly af-flicted.
11 I said' in my haste,
A'"ll men are liars.
12 What shall I render' unto the LORD
For' all his bene-fits toward͜ me?
13 I will take the cup' of sal-vation,
And call up'on the name of the͜ LORD.
14 I will pay my vows' unto the LORD
Now in the' presence of all his people.
15 Precious in the' sight of the͜ Lord
Is the' dëath of his saints.
16 O LORD, truly I' am thy servant;
I am thy servant, and the son of thine handmaid';
thou hast loosed my bonds.
17 I will offer to thee the' sacrifice of thanksgiving,
And will call up'on the name of the͜ LORD.
18 I will pay my vows' unto the LORD
Now in the' presence of all his people.

19 In the courts of the LORD's house, in the midst of'
thee, O Jerusalem.
Pr'äise ye the LORD.

PSALM CXVII.

O PRAISE the LORD', all ye nations:
Pr'aise him, all ye people.
2 For his merciful kindness is' great toward us;
And the truth of the LORD endureth for ever'.
Präise ye the LORD.

PSALM CXVIII.

O GIVE thanks unto the LORD; for' he is good;
Because his' mercy en-dureth for ever.
2 Let' Israel now say,
That his' mercy en-dureth for ever.
3 Let the house of' Aaron now say,
That his' mercy en-dureth for ever.
4 Let them now that' fear the_LORD say,
That his' mercy en-dureth for ever.
5 I called upon the LORD' in dis-tress:
The LORD answered me, and' set me in a_large place.
6 The LORD is' on my side;
I will not fear: what' can man do un-to_me?
7 The LORD taketh my part with' them that help_me:
Therefore shall I see my de'sire upon them that hate_me.
8 It is better to' trust in the_LORD,
Than' to put confidence in man.
9 It is better to' trust in the_LORD,
Than' to put confidence in princes.
10 All nations compassed' me a-bout:
But in the name of the' LORD will I de-stroy_them.

PSALMS.

11 They compassed me about; yea, they compassed'
me a-bout:
But in the name of the' LORD I will de-stroy͜them.
12 They compassed me about like bees; they are
quenched as the' fire of thorns:
For in the name of the' LORD I will de-stroy͜them.
13 Thou hast thrust sore at me, that' I might fall:
But the' LÖRD help-ed me.
14 The LORD is my' strength and song,
And is be'cöme my sal-vation.
15 The voice of rejoicing and salvation is in the' tabernacles of the͜righteous:
The right hand of the' LÖRD do-eth valiantly.
16 The right hand of the' LORD is exalted:
The right hand of the' LÖRD do-eth valiantly.
17 I shall not' die, but live,
And de'clare the works of the͜LORD.
18 The LORD hath' chastened me sore:
But he hath not' given me over unto death.
19 Open to me the' gates of righteousness:
I will go into them, and' I will praise the LORD:
20 This' gate of the͜LORD,
Into' which the righteous shall enter.
21 I will praise thee; for' thou hast heard͜me,
And art be'cöme my sal-vation.
22 The stone which the' builders re-fused
Is become the' head stone of the corner.
23 This is the' LÖRD's doing;
It is' marvel-lous in our eyes.
24 This is the day which the' LORD hath made:
We will re'joice and be͜glad in it.
25 Save now, I be'seech͜thee, O LORD!
O LORD, I be'seech͜thee, send now pros-perity.
26 Blessed be he that cometh in the' name of the͜ LORD:
We have blessed you' out͜of the house of the͜LORD.
27 God is the LORD, which hath' showed us light;
Bind the sacrifice with cords, even' unto the horns
of the͜altar.

PSALMS.

28 Thou art my God, and' I will praise‿thee;
Thou art my' God, I will ex-alt‿thee.
29 O give thanks unto the Lord; for' he is good:
For his' mercy en-dureth for ever.

PSALM CXIX.

ALEPH.

B LESSED are the undefiled' in the way,
Who walk in the' läw of the Lord.
2 Blessed are they that' keep his testimonies,
And that' seek him with the‿whole heart.
3 They also do' no in-iquity:
They' wälk in his ways.
4 Thou' hast com-manded‿us
To' keep thy pre-cepts diligently.
5 O that my ways' were di-rected
To' keep thy statutes!
6 Then shall I not' be a-shamed,
When I have respect unto' äll thy com-mandments.
7 I will praise thee with up'rightness of heart,
When I shall have' learned thy right-eous judgments.
8 I will' keep thy statutes:
O for'säke me not utterly.

BETH.

9 Wherewithal shall a young man' cleanse his way?
By taking heed thereto ac'cord-ing to thy word.
10 With my whole heart' have I sought‿thee:
O let me not' wander from thy com-mandments.
11 Thy word have I hid' in mine heart,
That I' might not sin a-gainst‿thee.
12 Blessed art' thou, O Lord:
T'each me thy statutes.
13 With my lips have' I de-clared
All the' judg-ments of thy mouth.

PSALMS.

14 I have rejoiced in the' way of‿thy testimonies
 As' much as in all riches.
15 I will meditate' in thy precepts,
 And have re'spect un-to thy ways.
16 I will delight myself' in thy statutes:
 I' will not forget thy word.

GIMEL.

17 Deal bountifully' with thy servant,
 That I may' live, and keep thy word.
18 Open' thou mine eyes,
 That I may behold' wondrous things out‿of thy law.
19 I am a' stranger in the‿earth;
 Hide not' thy com-mand-ments from‿me.
20 My soul breaketh for the longing' that it hath
 Unto thy' judgments at äll times.
21 Thou hast rebuked the' proud that‿are cursed,
 Which do' err from thy com-mandments.
22 Remove from me re'proach and contempt;
 For' I have kept thy testimonies.
23 Princes also did sit and' speak a-gainst‿me:
 But thy servant did' medi-tate in thy statutes.
24 Thy testimonies also are' my delight,
 A'ʼ̈nd my counsellors.

DALETH.

25 My soul cleaveth' unto the dust:
 Quicken thou me ac'cord-ing to thy word.
26 I have declared my ways', and thou heardest‿me:
 T̈each me thy statutes.
27 Make me to understand the' way of‿thy precepts:
 So shall I' talk of‿thy won-drous works.
28 My soul' melteth for heaviness:
 Strengthen thou me ac'cording un-to thy word.
29 Remove from me the' way of lying;
 And' grant me thy law graciously.
30 I have chosen the' way of truth:
 Thy judgments' have I laid be-fore‿me.

PSALMS.

31 I have stuck' unto thy testimonies:
O LORD', put me not to shame.
32 I will run the way of' thy com-mandments,
When thou' shalt en-large my heart.

HE.

33 Teach me, O LORD, the' way of thy statutes,
And I shall' keep it unto the end.
34 Give me understanding, and I shall' keep thy law;
Yea, I shall ob'serve it with my whole heart.
35 Make me to go in the path of' thy com-mandments;
For there'in do I de-light.
36 Incline my heart' unto thy testimonies,
And' not to covet-ous-ness.
37 Turn away mine eyes from be'hold-ing vanity;
And quicken' thou me in thy way.
38 Stablish thy word' unto thy servant,
Who is de'vot-ed to thy fear.
39 Turn away my reproach' which I fear:
For' thÿ judgments are good.
40 Behold, I have longed' after thy precepts:
Quicken' më in thy righteousness.

VAU.

41 Let thy mercies come also unto' me, O LORD;
Even thy salvation, ac'cord-ing to thy word.
42 So shall I have wherewith to answer' him that reproacheth me:
For I' trüst in thy word.
43 And take not the word of truth utterly' out of my mouth;
For I have' hop-ed in thy judgments.
44 So shall I' keep thy law
Con'tinually for ever and ever.
45 And I will' walk at liberty:
F'or I seek thy precepts.
46 I will speak of thy testimonies also be'fòre kings,
And' will not be a-shamed.

PSALMS.

47 And I will delight myself in' thy com-mandments,
  Wh'ĭch I have loved.
48 My hands also will I lift up unto thy command-
    ments, which' I have loved;
  And I will' medi-tate in thy statutes.

ZAIN.

49 Remember the word' unto thy servant,
  Upon which thou hast' caus-ed me to hope.
50 This is my comfort in' my af-fliction:
  F'or thy word hath quickened me.
51 The proud have had me' greatly in derision;
  Yet have I not de'clin-ed from thy law.
52 I remembered thy judgments of' old, O LORD;
  A'nd have comforted my-self.
53 Horror hath taken' hold up-on me,
  Because of the wicked' that for-sake thy law.
54 Thy statutes have' been my songs
  In the' house of my pilgrimage.
55 I have remembered thy name, O LORD', in the
    night,
  A'nd have kept thy law.
56 Th'is I had,
  Be'cause I kept thy precepts.

CHETH.

57 Thou art my' portion, O LORD:
  I have said that' I would keep thy words.
58 I entreated thy favour with' my whole heart:
  Be merciful unto me ac'cord-ing to thy word.
59 I' thought on my ways,
  And turned my' feet un-to thy testimonies.
60 I' mäde haste,
  And delayed not to' këep thy com-mandments.
61 The bands of the' wicked have robbed me:
  But I have' not for-gotten thy law.
62 At midnight I will rise to give' thanks unto thee,
  Because' of thy right-eous judgments.

PSALMS.

63 I am a companion of all' them that fear thee,
   And of' them that keep thy precepts.
64 The earth, O Lord, is' full of thy mercy:
   T'each me thy statutes.

TETH.

65 Thou hast dealt well with thy' servant, O Lord,
   Ac'cording un-to thy word.
66 Teach me good' judgment and knowledge:
   For I have be'liev-ed thy com-mandments.
67 Before I was afflicted I' went a-stray:
   But now' have I kept thy word.
68 Thou art good, and' do-est good;
   T'each me thy statutes.
69 The proud have forged a' lie a-gainst me:
   But I will keep thy' precepts with my whole heart.
70 Their heart is as' fat as grease;
   But I de'light in thy law.
71 It is good for me that I have' been af-flicted;
   That' I might learn thy statutes.
72 The law of thy mouth is' better unto me
   Than' thousands of gold and silver.

JOD.

73 Thy hands have' made me and fashioned me:
   Give me understanding, that I may' learn thy
      com-mandments.
74 They that fear thee will be glad' when they
      see me;
   Because I have' hop-ed in thy word.
75 I know, O Lord, that thy' judgments are right,
   And that thou in' faithful-ness hast af-flicted me.
76 Let, I pray thee, thy merciful kindness be' for my
      comfort,
   According to thy' word un-to thy servant.
77 Let thy tender mercies come unto me, that' I may
      live:
   For thy' law is my de-light.

PSALMS.

78 Let the proud be ashamed; for they dealt per-
veisely with me with'out a cause:
But I will' medi-tate in thy precepts.
79 Let those that fear thee' turn unto me,
And' those that have known thy testimonies.
80 Let my heart be sound' in thy statutes,
That' I be not a-shamed.

CAPH.

81 My soul fainteth for' thy sal-vation;
But I' höpe in thy word.
82 Mine eyes fail' for thy word,
Saying', Whën wilt thou comfort me?
83 For I am become like a' bottle in the smoke;
Yet do I' not for-get thy statutes.
84 How many are the' days of thy servant?
When wilt thou execute' judgment on them that
persecute me?
85 The proud have digged' pits for me,
Which' are not after thy law.
86 All thy com'mandments are faithful:
They persecute me' wrong-fully; help thou me.
87 They had almost consumed me' up-on earth;
But' I for-sook not thy precepts.
88 Quicken me after' thy loving-kindness;
So shall I keep the' testi-mony of thy mouth.

LAMED.

89 For' ever, O Lord,
Thy' word is settled in heaven.
90 Thy faithfulness is unto' all gene-rations;
Thou hast established the' earth, and it a-bideth.
91 They continue this day according' to thine ordinances:
For' äll are thy servants.
92 Unless thy law had been' my de-lights,
I should then have' perished in mine af-fliction.

PSALMS.

93 I will never for′get thy precepts;
 For′ with them thou hast quickened‿me.
94 I am′ thīne, save‿me;
 For′ I have sought thy precepts.
95 The wicked have waited for me′, to de-stroy‿me:
 But I′ will con-sider thy testimonies.
96 I have seen an end of′ all per-fection:
 But thy commandment′ is ex-ceed-ing broad.

MEM.

97 O how love′ I thy law!
 It is my medi′ta-tion all the day.
98 Thou through thy commandments hast made me′
  wiser than mine‿enemies:
 For′ they are ev-er with‿me.
99 I have more understanding than′ all my teachers:
 For thy testimonies′ are my me-di-tation.
100 I understand′ more than the‿ancients,
 Be′cause I keep thy precepts.
101 I have refrained my feet from every′ e-vil way,
 That′ I might keep thy word.
102 I have not departed′ from thy judgments:
 För thou hast taught‿me.
103 How sweet are thy words′ unto my taste!
 Yea, sweeter than′ ho-ney to my mouth!
104 Through thy precepts I′ get under-standing:
 Therefore I′ häte every false way.

NUN.

105 Thy word is a lamp′ unto my feet,
 And a′ lĭght unto my path.
106 I have sworn, and I′ will per-form‿it,
 That I will′ keep thy right-eous judgments.
107 I am afflicted′ ve-ry much:
 Quicken me, O Lord, ac′cording un-to thy word.
108 Accept, I beseech thee, the freewill offerings of
  my′ mouth, O Lord,
 And′ tëach me thy judgments.

PSALMS.

109 My soul is continually' in my hand:
   Yet do I' not for-get thy law.
110 The wicked have laid a' snare for me:
   Yet I' erred not from thy precepts.
111 Thy testimonies have I taken as an' heritage for ever:
   For they are the re'joic-ing of my heart.
112 I have inclined mine heart to per'form thy statutes
   Alway', even un-to the end.

SAMECH.

113 I' hate vain thoughts:
   But' thy law do I love.
114 Thou art my hiding-place' and my shield:
   I' hope in thy word.
115 Depart from me, ye' e-vil-doers:
   For I will keep the com'mand-ments of my God.
116 Uphold me according unto thy word, that' I may live;
   And let me not be a'sham-ed of my hope.
117 Hold thou me up, and I' shall be safe;
   And I will have respect un'to thy statutes con-tinually.
118 Thou hast trodden down all them that' err from thy statutes:
   For' their de-ceit is falsehood.
119 Thou puttest away all the wicked of the' earth like dross:
   Therefore' I love thy testimonies.
120 My flesh trembleth for' fear of thee;
   And I am a'fraid of thy judgments.

AIN.

121 I have done' judgment and justice:
   Leave me' not to mine op-pressors.
122 Be surety for thy' servant for good:
   Let' not the proud op-press me.
123 Mine eyes fail for' thy sal-vation,
   And for the' word of thy righteousness.

PSALMS.

124 Deal with thy servant according' unto thy mercy,
  And' tĕach me thy statutes.
125 I' am thy servant;
  Give me understanding, that' I may know thy testimonies.
126 It is time for thee', LORD, to work:
  For they' have made void thy law.
127 Therefore I love thy commandments a'bŏve gold;
  Yea', abŏve fine gold.
128 Therefore I esteem all thy precepts concerning all things' to be right;
  And I' häte every false way.

PE.

129 Thy' testimonies are wonderful:
  Therefore' doth my sŏul keep⁀them.
130 The entrance of thy' words giveth light;
  It giveth under'standing un-to the simple.
131 I opened my' mouth, and panted:
  For I' longed for thy com-mandments.
132 Look thou upon me, and be' merciful un-to⁀me,
  As thou usest to do unto' those that love thy name.
133 Order my steps' in thy word:
  And let not any iniquity' have do-min-ion over⁀me.
134 Deliver me from the op'pression of man;
  So' will I keep thy precepts.
135 Make thy face to shine up'on thy servant;
  And' tĕach me thy statutes.
136 Rivers of water run' down mine eyes,
  Be'cause they keep⁀not thy law.

TZADDI.

137 Righteous art' thou, O LORD,
  And' up-right are thy judgments.
138 Thy testimonies that' thou hast commanded
  Are' righteous and ve-ry faithful.

PSALMS.

139 My' zeal hath consumed me,
    Because mine enemies' have for-gotten thy words.
140 Thy word is' ve-ry pure:
    There'fore thy ser-vant loveth it.
141 I am small' and de-spised:
    Yet do not' I for-get thy precepts.
142 Thy righteousness is an ever'last-ing righteousness,
    And thy' law is the truth.
143 Trouble and anguish have' taken hold on me:
    Yet thy com'mandments are my de-lights.
144 The righteousness of thy testimonies' is ever-lasting:
    Give me under'standing, and I shall live.

KOPH.

145 I cried with my whole heart'; hear me, O LORD:
    I' will keep thy statutes.
146 I' cried un-to thee:
    Save me, and' I shall keep thy testimonies.
147 I prevented the dawning of the' morning, and cried:
    I' hoped in thy word.
148 Mine eyes pre'vent the night watches,
    That I might' medi-tate in thy word.
149 Hear my voice, according unto' thy loving-kindness:
    O LORD, quicken me ac'cord-ing to thy judgment.
150 They draw nigh that follow' af-ter mischief:
    They are' far from thy law.
151 Thou art' near, O LORD;
    And all' thy com-mandments are truth.
152 Concerning thy testimonies, I have' known of old
    That thou hast' found-ed them for ever.

RESH.

153 Consider mine affliction', and de-liver me:
    For I' do not forget thy law.
154 Plead my cause', and de-liver me:
    Quicken me ac'cord-ing to thy word.
155 Salvation is' far from the wicked:
    For they' seek not thy statutes.

160

PSALMS.

156 Great are thy tender' mercies, O LORD;
   Quicken me ac'cord-ing to thy judgments.
157 Many are my persecutors' and mine enemies;
   Yet do I not de'cline from thy testimonies.
158 I beheld the transgressors', and was grieved;
   Because' they kept not thy word.
159 Consider how I' love thy precepts:
   Quicken me, O LORD, ac'cording to thy loving-kindness.
160 Thy word is true' from the‿be-ginning:
   And every one of thy righteous' judgments en-dureth for ever.

SCHIN.

161 Princes have persecuted me with'out a cause:
   But my heart' standeth in awe of‿thy word.
162 I rejoice' at thy word,
   As' one that findeth great spoil.
163 I hate and ab'hor lying;
   But' thy law do I love.
164 Seven times a day' do I praise‿thee
   Because' of thy right-eous judgments.
165 Great peace have they which' love thy law:
   And' noth-ing shall of-fend‿them.
166 LORD, I have hoped for' thy sal-vation,
   A'nd done thy com-mandments.
167 My soul hath' kept thy testimonies;
   And' I love them ex-ceedingly.
168 I have kept thy precepts' and thy testimonies:
   For all my' ways are be-fore‿thee.

TAU.

169 Let my cry come near before' thee, O LORD:
   Give me understanding ac'cord-ing to thy word
170 Let my supplication' come be-fore‿thee:
   Deliver me ac'cord-ing to thy word.
171 My lips shall' ut-ter praise,
   When thou hast' taught me thy statutes.

PSALMS.

172 My tongue shall speak' of thy word:
　　For all' thy com-mandments are righteousness.
173 Let' thine hand help me;
　　For' I have chosen thy precepts.
174 I have longed for thy sal'vation, O LORD;
　　And thy' law is my de-light.
175 Let my soul live, and' it shall praise thee;
　　And' let thy judg-ments help me.
176 I have gone astray like a lost sheep': seek thy servant;
　　For I do not for'gët thy com-mandments.

PSALM CXX.

¶ A Song of degrees.

IN my distress I cried un'to the LORD,
　　A'''nd he heard me.
2 Deliver my soul, O LORD, from' ly-ing lips,
　　And' from a de-ceit-ful tongue.
3 What shall be given' un-to thee?
　　Or what shall be done un'to thee, thou false tongue?
4 Sharp' arrows of the mighty,
　　With' cö als of juniper.
5 Woe is me that I' sojourn in Mesech,
　　That I' dwell in the tents of Kedar!
6 My soul hath long' dwelt with him
　　That' hä't-eth peace.
7 I' am for peace:
　　But when I' speak, they are for war.

PSALM CXXI.

¶ A Song of degrees.

I WILL lift up mine eyes un'to the hills,
　　From' whënce cometh my help.
2 My help cometh' from the LORD,
　　Which' mäde heaven and earth.

PSALMS.

3 He will not suffer thy foot' to be moved:
 He that' keepeth thee will not slumber.
4 Behold, he that' keep-eth Israel
 Shall' nei-ther slumber nor sleep.
5 The Lord' is thy keeper:
 The Lord is thy' shade up-on thy right‿hand.
6 The sun shall not' smite‿thee by day,
 N'or the moon by night.
7 The Lord shall preserve thee' from all evil:
 He' shall pre-serve thy soul.
8 The Lord shall preserve thy going out and' thy coming in,
 From this time forth, and' even for ev-er-more.

PSALM CXXII.

A Song of degrees of David.

I WAS glad when they' said un-to‿me,
 Let us go' into the house of the‿Lord.
2 Our feet shall stand with'in thy gates,
 O'''' Je-rusalem.
3 Jerusalem is builded' as a city
 That' is com-pact to-gether:
4 Whither the tribes go up, the' tribes of the‿Lord,
 Unto the testimony of Israel, to give thanks' unto the name of the‿Lord.
5 For there are set' thrones of judgment,
 The' thrones of the‿house of David.
6 Pray for the peace' of Je-rusalem:
 Th'ey shall prosper that love‿thee.
7 Peace be with'in thy walls,
 And pros'perity with-in thy palaces.
8 For my brethren and com'pa-nions' sakes,
 I will now say', Peace be with-in‿thee.
9 Because of the house of the' Lord our God
 I' will seek thy good.

PSALMS.

PSALM CXXIII.
¶ A Song of degrees.

UNTO thee lift I' up mine eyes,
O thou that' dwell-est in the heavens.
2 Behold, as the eyes of servants look unto the hand
of their masters, and as the eyes of a maiden
unto the hand' of her mistress;
So our eyes wait upon the LORD our God, until
that' he have mercy up-on‿us.
3 Have mercy upon us, O LORD, have' mercy
up-on‿us:
For we are exceedingly' fill-ed with con-tempt.
4 Our soul is exceedingly filled with the scorning of
those that' are at ease,
And' with the‿con-tempt of the‿proud.

PSALM CXXIV.
¶ A Song of degrees of David.

IF it had not been the LORD who was' on our side,
Now' mäy Is-rael say;
2 If it had not been the LORD who was' on our side,
When' men rose up a-gainst‿us;
3 Then they had swallowed' us up quick,
When their' wrath was kindled a-gainst‿us:
4 Then the waters had' o-ver-whelmed‿us,
The stream had' göne over our soul:
5 Then the' pröud waters
H'ad gone over our soul.
6 Blessed' be the LORD,
Who hath not given us as a' prëy to their teeth.
7 Our soul is escaped as a bird out of the' snare of
the‿fowlers:
The snare is broken, and' wĕ are es-caped.
8 Our help is in the' name of the‿LORD,
Who' mäde heaven and earth.

PSALMS.

PSALM CXXV.
¶ A Song of degrees.

THEY that trust in the LORD shall be' as mount Zion,
Which cannot be removed', but a-bideth for ever.
2 As the mountains are round a'bout Je-rusalem,
So the LORD is round about his people from' henceforth even for ever.
3 For the rod of the wicked shall not rest upon the' lot of the‿righteous;
Lest the righteous put forth their' hands un-to in-iquity.
4 Do good, O LORD, unto those' that be good,
And to them that are' up-right in their hearts.
5 As for such as turn aside unto their' crook-ed ways,
The LORD shall lead them forth with the workers of iniquity: but' peace shall be upon Israel.

PSALM CXXVI.
¶ A Song of degrees.

WHEN the LORD turned again the cap'tivity of Zion,
We' were like them that dream.
2 Then was our mouth filled with laughter, and our' tongue with singing:
Then said they among the heathen, The LORD hath' döne great things for‿them.
3 The LORD hath done' great things for‿us;
Wh'ere-of we are glad.
4 Turn again our cap'tivity, O LORD,
As the' strëams in the south.
5 They that' sow in tears
Shall' rë"ap in joy.

PSALMS.

6 He that goeth forth and weepeth, bearing' pre-cious seed,
Shall doubtless come again with rejoicing', bringing his shëaves with him.

PSALM CXXVII.
¶ ·A Song of degrees for Solomon.

EXCEPT the LORD build the house, they labour in' vain that build it:
Except the LORD keep the city, the watchman' wak-eth but in vain.
2 It is vain for you to rise up early, to sit up late, to eat the' bread of sorrows:
For so he' giveth his belov-ed sleep.
3 Lo, children are an' heritage of the LORD:
And the fruit of the' womb is his re-ward.
4 As arrows are in the hand of a' might-y man;
So are' child-ren of the youth.
5 Happy is the man that hath his' quiver full of them:
They shall not be ashamed, but they shall speak with the' ene-mies in the gate.

PSALM CXXVIII.
¶ A Song of degrees.

BLESSED is every one that' feareth the LORD;
That' walk-eth in his ways.
2 For thou shalt eat the labour' of thine hands:
Happy shalt thou be, and it' shall be well with thee.
3 Thy wife shall be as a fruitful vine by the sides' of thine house:
Thy children like olive plants' round a-bout thy table.
4 Behold, that thus shall the' man be blessed
Th'at feareth the LORD.

PSALMS.

5 The Lord shall bless thee' out of Zion:
And thou shalt see the good of Jerusalem' all
the‿days of thy life.
6 Yea, thou shalt see thy' child-ren's children,
And' pëace up-on Israel.

PSALM CXXIX.
¶ A Song of degrees.

MANY a time have they afflicted me' from my youth,
May' Is-ra-el now say:
2 Many a time have they afflicted me' from my youth;
Yet they' have‿not pre-vailed a-gainst‿me.
3 The plowers plowed up'on my back;
They' mäde long their furrows.
4 The' Lord is righteous:
He hath cut a'sunder the cords of the‿wicked.
5 Let them all' be con-founded
And' turned back that hate Zion.
6 Let them be as the grass up'on the housetops,
Which withereth a'fore it grow-eth up;
7 Wherewith the mower filleth' not his hand,
Nor he that' bind-eth sheaves his bosom.
8 Neither do they which' go by say,
The blessing of the Lord be upon you: we bless
you in the' näme of the Lord.

PSALM CXXX.
¶ A Song of degrees.

OUT' of the depths
Have I cried' un-to thee, O Lord.
2 Lord', hear my voice;
Let thine ears be attentive to the' voice of my
sup-plications.
3 If thou, Lord, shouldst' mark in-iquities,
O' Lörd, who shall stand?

PSALMS.

4 But there is for'giveness with thee,
That' thöu mayest be feared.
5 I wait for the LORD, my' soul doth wait,
And in his' wörd do I hope.
6 My soul waiteth for the LORD more than they that'
watch for the morning;
I say, more than they that' wätch for the morning.
7 Let Israel' hope in the LORD:
For with the LORD there is mercy, and with' him
is plenteous re-demption.
8 And he shall re'dĕem Israel
Fr'om all his in-iquities.

PSALM CXXXI.

¶ A Song of degrees of David.

LORD, my heart is not haughty, nor mine' ëyes
lofty:
Neither do I exercise myself in great matters, or'
in things too high for me.
2 Surely I have behaved and quieted myself, as a
child that is weaned' of his mother:
My soul is even' as a wean-ed child.
3 Let Israel' hope in the LORD,
From' hence-forth and for ever.

PSALM CXXXII.

¶ A Song of degrees.

LORD, re'mem-ber David,
And' äll his af-flictions:
2 How he sware un'to the LORD,
And vowed unto the' might-y God of Jacob;
3 Surely I will not come into the tabernącle' of my
house,
Nor' go up into my bed;

PSALMS.

4 I will not give sleep' to mine eyes,
   Or' slum-ber to mine eyelids,
5 Until I find out a' place for the␣Lord,
   An habitation for the' might-y God of Jacob.
6 Lo, we heard of' it at Ephratah;
   We found it in the' fields of the wood.
7 We will go' into his tabernacles;
   We will' wor-ship at his footstool.
8 Arise, O Lord', into thy rest;
   Thou, and the' ärk of thy strength.
9 Let thy priests be' clothed with righteousness;
   And let thy' säints shout for joy.
10 For thy servant' Da-vid's sake
   Turn not away the' face of thine an-ointed.
11 The Lord hath sworn in truth unto David, he
      will' not turn from␣it,
   Of the fruit of thy body will I' set up-on thy
      throne.
12 If thy children will keep my covenant and my tes-
      timony that' I shall teach␣them,
   Their children shall also sit upon thy' throne for
      ev-er-more.
13 For the Lord hath' chos-en Zion;
   He hath desired it' for his ha-bi-tation.
14 This is my' rest for ever:
   Here will I dwell'; for I have de-sired␣it.
15 I will abundantly' bless her provision:
   I will' satisfy her poor with bread.
16 I will also clothe her priests' with sal-vation;
   And her saints shall' shout a-loud for joy.
17 There will I make the horn of' David to bud:
   I have ordained a' lamp for mine an-ointed.
18 His enemies will I' clothe with shame;
   But upon him'self shall his crown flourish.

PSALMS.

PSALM CXXXIII.
¶ A Song of degrees of David.

BEHOLD, how good and how' pleasant it is
For brethren to' dwell to-gether in unity!
2 It is like the precious ointment upon the head, that ran down upon the beard, even' Aa-ron's beard;
That went down to the' skïrts of his garments;
3 As the dew of Hermon, and as the dew that descended upon the' mountains of Zion:
For there the LORD commanded the blessing, even' life for ev-er-more.

PSALM CXXXIV.
¶ A Song of degrees.

BEHOLD, bless ye the LORD, all ye' servants of the‿LORD,
Which by night stand in the' höuse of the LORD.
2 Lift up your' hands in the‿sanctuary,
And' blë̈ss the LORD.
3 The LORD that made' heaven and earth
Bl'ess thee out of Zion.

PSALM CXXXV.

PRAISE' ye the LORD.
Praise ye the name of the LORD; praise him, O ye' ser-vants of the LORD.
2 Ye that stand in the' house of the‿LORD,
In the courts of the' höuse of our God,
3 Praise the LORD; for the' LORD is good:
Sing praises unto his' name; for it is pleasant.
4 For the LORD hath chosen Jacob' unto him-self,
And Israel for' his pe-cu-liar treasure.
5 For I know that the' LORD is great,
And that our' LORD is above all gods.

PSALMS.

6 Whatsoever the LORD pleased, that did' he in heaven,
And in earth, in the' seas, and all deep places.
7 He causeth the vapours to ascend from the' ends of the earth;
He maketh lightnings for the rain; he bringeth the' wind out of his treasuries.
8 Who smote the' firstborn of Egypt,
B'oth of man and beast.
9 Who sent tokens and wonders into the midst of' thee, O Egypt,
Upon Pharaoh', and upon all his servants.
10 Who' smote great nations,
And' slëw might-y kings;
11 Sihon king of the Amorites, and Og' king of Bashan,
And' all the kingdoms of Canaan;
12 And gave their' land for an heritage,
An heritage' un-to Israel his people.
13 Thy name, O LORD, en'dureth for ever;
And thy memorial, O LORD', through-out all generations.
14 For the LORD will' judge his people,
And he will repent him'self con-cerning his servants.
15 The idols of the heathen are' silver and gold,
The' wörk of men's hands.
16 They have mouths', but they speak not;
Eyes' have they, but they see not;
17 They have ears', but they hear not;
Neither is there' any breath in their mouths.
18 They that make them are' like un-to them:
So is' every one that trust-eth in them.
19 Bless the LORD, O' house of Israel:
Bless the' LORD, O house of Aaron:
20 Bless the LORD, O' house of Levi:
Ye that' fear the LORD, bless the LORD.
21 Blessed be the LORD out of Zion, which' dwelleth at Jerusalem.
Pr'äise ye the LORD.

171

PSALMS.

PSALM CXXXVI.

O GIVE thanks unto the LORD; for' he is good:
 For his' mercy en-dureth for ever.
2 O give thanks unto the' God of gods:
 For his' mercy en-dureth for ever.
3 O give thanks to the' LORD of lords:
 For his' mercy en-dureth for ever.
4 To him who alone' doeth great wonders:
 For his' mercy en-dureth for ever.
5 To him that by wisdom' made the heavens:
 For his' mercy en-dureth for ever.
6 To him that stretched out the earth a'bove the waters:
 For his' mercy en-dureth for ever.
7 To him that' made great lights:
 For his' mercy en-dureth for ever:
8 The sun to' rule by day:
 For his' mercy en-dureth for ever:
9 The moon and stars to' rule by night:
 For his' mercy en-dureth for ever.
10 To him that smote Egypt' in their firstborn:
 For his' mercy en-dureth for ever:
11 And brought out Israel' from a-mong‿them:
 For his' mercy en-dureth for ever:
12 With a strong hand, and with a' stretched out arm:
 For his' mercy en-dureth for ever.
13 To him which divided the Red Sea' in-to parts:
 For his' mercy en-dureth for ever:
14 And made Israel to pass' through the midst‿of‿it:
 For his' mercy en-dureth for ever:
15 But overthrew Pharaoh and his host' in the‿Red Sea,
 For his' mercy en-dureth for ever.
16 To him which led his people' through the wilderness:
 For his' mercy en-dureth for ever.

17 To him which' smote great kings:
  For his' mercy en-dureth for ever:
18 And slew' fa-mous kings:
  For his' mercy en-dureth for ever:
19 Sihon' king of the Amorites:
  For his' mercy en-dureth for ever:
20 And Og the' king of Bashan:
  For his' mercy en-dureth for ever:
21 And gave their' land for an heritage:
  For his' mercy en-dureth for ever:
22 Even an heritage unto' Israel his servant:
  For his' mercy en-dureth for ever.
23 Who remembered us in our' low es-tate:
  For his' mercy en-dureth for ever:
24 And hath redeemed us' from our enemies:
  For his' mercy en-dureth for ever.
25 Who giveth food to' äll flesh:
  For his' mercy en-dureth for ever.
26 O give thanks unto the' God of heaven:
  For his' mercy en-dureth for ever.

PSALM CXXXVII.

BY the rivers of Babylon, there we sat down', yea,
  we wept,
  When' we re-member-ed Zion.
2 We' hanged our harps
  Upon the willows' in the midst there-of.
3 For there they that carried us away captive
    required of' us a song;
  And they that wasted us required of us mirth,
    saying, Sing us' one of the songs of Zion.
4 How' shall we sing
  The' LORD's song in a strange land?
5 If I forget thee', O Je-rusalem,
  Let my right' hand for-get her cunning.

PSALMS.

6 If I do not remember thee, let my tongue cleave to
the' roof of my mouth;
If I prefer not Jerusalem a'böve my chief joy.
7 Remember, O LORD, the children of Edom in the
day' of Je-rusalem;
Who said, Rase it, rase it, even' to the foun-dation
there-of.
8 O daughter of Babylon, who art to' be de-stroyed:
Happy shall he be that rewardeth thee as' thou
hast serv-ed us.
9 Happy' shall he be
That taketh and dasheth thy' little ones a-gainst the
stones.

PSALM CXXXVIII.
¶ A Psalm of David.

I WILL praise thee with' my whole heart:
Before the gods will I' sing praise un-to thee.
2 I will worship toward thy holy temple, and praise
thy name for thy lovingkindness and' for thy
truth:
For thou hast magnified thy' word above all thy
name.
3 In the day when I' cried thou answeredst me,
And strengthenedst me with' strëngth in my soul.
4 All the kings of the earth shall' praise thee, O
LORD,
When they hear the' wörds of thy mouth.
5 Yea, they shall sing in the' ways of the LORD:
For great is the' glo-ry of the LORD.
6 Though the LORD be high, yet hath he respect'
unto the lowly:
But the proud he' know-eth afär off.
7 Though I walk in the midst of trouble', thou wilt
revive me:
Thou shalt stretch forth thine hand against the
wrath of mine enemies, and' thy right hand
shall save me.

8 The LORD will perfect that' which con-cerneth‿me:
  Thy mercy, O LORD, endureth for ever: forsake
  not the' works of thine own hands.

PSALM CXXXIX.

¶ To the chief Musician, A Psalm of David.

O LORD', thou hast searched‿me,
  A'‿nd knöwn me.
2 Thou knowest my downsitting and' mine up-rising;
  Thou understandest my' thought a-fär off.
3 Thou compassest my path and my' ly-ing down,
  And art ac'quainted with all my ways.
4 For there is not a word' in my tongue,
  But, lo, O LORD, thou' knowest it al-to-gether.
5 Thou hast beset me' behind and before,
  And' laid thine hand up-on‿me.
6 Such knowledge is too' wonder-ful for‿me;
  It is high, I' cannot at-tain un-to‿it.
7 Whither shall I go' from thy spirit?
  Or whither shall I' flëe from thy presence?
8 If I ascend up into heaven', thou art there:
  If I make my bed in hell, be'höld, thou art there.
9 If I take the' wings of the‿morning,
  And dwell in the' utter-most parts of the‿sea;
10 Even there shall' thy hand lead‿me,
  A'nd thy right‿hand shall hold‿me.
11 If I say, Surely the' darkness shall cover‿me;
  Even the night' shall be light a-bout‿me.
12 Yea, the darkness hideth not from thee; but the
    night' shineth as the‿day:
  The darkness and the light are' both a-like to thee.
13 For thou hast pos'sessed my reins:
  Thou hast covered me' in my mo-ther's womb.
14 I will praise thee; for I am fearfully and' wonder-
    fully made:
  Marvellous are thy works; and that my' söul
    knoweth right well.

PSALMS.

15 My substance was not hid from thee, when I was'
made in secret,
And curiously wrought in the' low-est parts of
the_earth.
16 Thine eyes did see my substance, yet' being un-
perfect;
And in thy book all my members were written,
which in continuance were fashioned, when as'
yet there was none of_them.
17 How precious also are thy thoughts unto' me, O
God!
How' great is the_sum of them!
18 If I should count them, they are more in number'
than the sand:
When I awake', I am still with thee.
19 Surely thou wilt slay the' wicked, O God:
Depart from me', therefore, ye blood-y men.
20 For they speak a'gainst thee wickedly,
And thine enemies' take thy name in vain.
21 Do not I hate them, O LORD, that' häte thee?
And am not I grieved with those that' rise up
a-gainst_thee?
22 I hate them with' per-fect hatred:
I' count them mine enemies.
23 Search me, O God, and' know my heart:
Try' me, and know my thoughts;
24 And see if there be any wicked' way in me,
And lead me' in the way ever-lasting.

PSALM CXL.

¶ To the chief Musician,'A Psalm of David.

DELIVER me, O LORD, from the' e-vil man:
Preserve me' from the vio-lent man;
2 Which imagine mischiefs' in their heart:
Continually are they' gathered to-gether for war.
3 They have sharpened their' tongues like a_serpent:
Adder's' poison is under their lips. Selah.

PSALMS.

4 Keep me, O Lord, from the' hands of the‿wicked;
   Preserve me from the violent man; who have pur-
      posed to' o-ver-throw my goings.
5 The proud have hid a snare' for‿me, and cords;
   They have spread a net by the way side'; they
      have set gins for‿me. Selah.
6 I said unto the Lord, Thou' art my God:
   Hear the voice of my' sup-pli-cations, O Lord.
7 O God the Lord, the strength of' my sal-vation,
   Thou hast covered my head' in the day of battle.
8 Grant not, O Lord, the de'sires of the‿wicked;
   Further not his wicked device', lest they exalt
      them-selves. Selah.
9 As for the head of those that compass' me a-bout,
   Let the mischief' of their own lips cover‿them.
10 Let burning coals fall upon them: let them be
      cast' into the fire;
   Into deep pits, that they' rise not up a-gain.
11 Let not an evil speaker be established' in the earth:
   Evil shall hunt the violent' man to o-ver-throw‿him.
12 I know that the Lord will maintain the cause' of
      the‿af-flicted,
   A'nd the right of the‿poor.
13 Surely the righteous shall give thanks' unto thy
      name;
   The upright shall' dwell in thy presence.

PSALM CXLI.

¶ A Psalm of David.

LORD, I cry unto thee: make' haste un-to‿me;
   Give ear unto my voice', when I cry un-to‿thee
2 Let my prayer be set forth be'fore‿thee as incense,
   And the lifting up of my hands' as the even-ing
      sacrifice.
3 Set a watch, O Lord, be'fore my mouth;
   Ke'ep the‿door of my lips.

PSALMS.

4 Incline not my heart to any evil thing, to practise wicked works with men that' work in-iquity; And let me not' ëat of their dainties.
5 Let the righteous smite me; it shall be a kindness: and let him reprove me; it shall be an' excellent oil,
Which shall not break my head: for yet my prayer also shall' be in their ca-lamities.
6 When their judges are overthrown in' sto-ny places, They shall hear my' words; for they are sweet.
7 Our bones are scattered at the' gräve's mouth, As when one cutteth and cleaveth' wood up-on the earth.
8 But mine eyes are unto thee, O' GOD the LORD: In thee is my trust', leave not my soul destitute.
9 Keep me from the snares which they have' laid for me,
And the gins of the' work-ers of in-iquity.
10 Let the wicked fall into' their own nets, Whilst that' I with-al es-cape.

PSALM CXLII.

*Maschil of David, A Prayer when he was in the cave.

I CRIED unto the LORD' with my voice;
With my voice unto the LORD did I' make my sup-pli-cation.
2 I poured out my com'plaint be-fore him; I' showed be-fore him my trouble.
3 When my spirit was overwhelmed within me, then thou' knewest my path;
In the way wherein I walked have they privily' laid a snäre for me.
4 I looked on my right hand, and beheld, but there was no man' that would know me:
Refuge failed me; no man' car-ed for my soul.

5 I cried unto thee, O' Lord: I said,
Thou art my refuge, and my portion' in the land of
the living.
6 Attend unto my cry; for I am' brought very
low:
Deliver me from my persecutors; for' they are
stronger than I.
7 Bring my soul out of prison, that I may' praise thy
name:
The righteous shall compass me about; for thou'
shalt deal bounti-fully with me.

PSALM CXLIII.

¶ A Psalm of David.

HEAR my prayer, O Lord; give ear to my' suppli-cations:
In thy faithfulness' answer me, and in thy
righteousness.
2 And enter not into judgment' with thy servant:
For in thy sight shall' no man living be justified.
3 For the enemy hath persecuted my soul; he hath
smitten my life' down to the ground:
He hath made me to dwell in darkness, as those
that' have been löng dead.
4 Therefore is my spirit over'whelmed with-in me:
My' heart with-in me is desolate.
5 I remember the days of old; I meditate on' all thy
works;
I muse on the' wörks of thy hands.
6 I stretch forth my' hands unto thee:
My soul thirsteth after thee', as a thirst-y land.
Selah.
7 Hear me speedily, O Lord; my' spir-it faileth:
Hide not thy face from me, lest I be like unto them
that' go down into the pit.

PSALMS.

8 Cause me to hear thy lovingkindness in the morning; for in thee' do I trust:
Cause me to know the way wherein I should walk; for I lift' up my soul un-to‿thee.
9 Deliver me, O Lord', from mine enemies:
I' flee unto thee to hide‿me.
10 Teach me to do thy will; for' thou‿art my God:
Thy spirit is good; lead me' into the land of uprightness.
11 Quicken me, O Lord, for' thy name's sake:
For thy righteousness' sake bring' my soul out of trouble.
12 And of thy mercy cut off mine enemies, and destroy all them that af'flict my soul:
Fo'r I am thy servant.

PSALM CXLIV.

¶ A Psalm of David.

BLESSED be the' Lord my strength,
Which teacheth my hands to war', and my fingers to fight:
2 My goodness, and my fortress; my high tower, and' my de-liverer;
My shield, and he in whom I trust; who sub'dueth my peo-ple under‿me.
3 Lord, what is man, that thou takest' knowledge of him!
Or the son of man, that thou' makest ac-count of him!
4 Man is' like to vanity:
His days are as a' shadow that passeth a-way.
5 Bow thy heavens, O Lord, and' come down:
Touch the' mountains, and they shall smoke.
6 Cast forth' lightning, and scatter‿them:
Shoot out thine' ar-rows, and de-stroy‿them.

PSALMS.

7 Send thine' hand from above;
   Rid me, and deliver me out of great waters, from the' hand of strange children;
8 Whose' mouth speaketh vanity,
   And their right hand' is‿a right hand of falsehood.
9 I will sing a new song unto' thee, O God:
   Upon a psaltery, and an instrument of ten strings, will' I sing praises un-to‿thee.
10 It is he that giveth salvation' un-to kings:
   Who delivereth David his servant' from the hurt-ful sword.
11 Rid me, and deliver me from the hand of' strange children,
   Whose mouth speaketh vanity, and their right hand' is‿a right hand of falsehood:
12 That our sons may be as plants grown up' in their youth;
   That our daughters may be as corner stones, polished after the si'mili-tude of a palace:
13 That our garners may be full, affording all' manner of store:
   That our sheep may bring forth thousands, and' ten thousands in our streets:
14 That our oxen may be' strong to labour;
   That there be no breaking in, nor going out; that there be no com'plain-ing in our streets.
15 Happy is that people that is in' such a case:
   Yea, happy is that people', whose God is the LORD.

PSALM CXLV.

¶ David's Psalm of Praise.

I WILL extol thee, my' God, O King;
   And I will bless thy' name for ever and ever.
2 Every day' will I bless‿thee;
   And I will praise thy' name for ever and ever.

PSALMS.

3 Great is the LORD, and greatly' to be praised:
  And his' great-ness is un-searchable.
4 One generation shall praise thy' works to another,
  And shall de'clare thy might-y acts.
5 I will speak of the glorious honour' of thy majesty,
  And' of thy won-drous works.
6 And men shall speak of the might of thy terri-ble acts:
  And I' will de-clare thy greatness.
7 They shall abundantly utter the memory of' thy great goodness,
  And shall sing of thy righteousness.
8 The LORD is gracious, and' full of compassion:
  Slow to' anger, and of great mercy.
9 The LORD is' good to all;
  And his tender mercies are' o-ver all his works.
10 All thy works shall' praise_thee, O LORD;
   A'nd thy saints shall bless_thee.
11 They shall speak of the glory' of thy kingdom,
   And talk of thy power;
12 To make known to the sons of men his' might-y acts,
   And the glorious' majes-ty of his kingdom.
13 Thy kingdom is an ever last-ing kingdom,
   And thy dominion endureth' through-out all gene-rations.
14 The LORD upholdeth' all that fall,
   And raiseth up all those that be bow-ed down.
15 The eyes of all' wait upon thee:
   And thou givest them their' meat in due season.
16 Thou' openest thine hand,
   And satisfiest the desire of' ev-ery liv-ing thing.
17 The LORD is righteous in' all his ways,
   And' holy in all his works.
18 The LORD is nigh unto all them that call up-on_him,
   To all that' call upon him in truth.

19 He will fulfil the desire of′ them that fear‿him:
He also will hear their′ crÿ, and will save‿them.
20 The Lord preserveth all′ them that love‿him:
But all the′ wicked will he de-stroy.
21 My mouth shall speak the′ praise of the‿Lord;
And let all flesh bless his holy′ name for ever and ever.

PSALM CXLVI.

PRAISE′ ye the Lord.
    Praise the′ Lörd, O my soul.
2 While I live will I′ praise the Lord:
I will sing praises unto my God′ while I have any being.
3 Put not your trust in princes, nor in the′ son of man,
In′ whom there is no help.
4 His breath goeth forth, he returneth′ to his earth:
In that very′ däy his thoughts perish.
5 Happy is he that hath the God of Jacob′ for his help,
Whose hope is′ in the Lord his God;
6 Which made heaven, and earth, the sea, and all that′ there-in is;
Which′ keep-eth truth for ever:
7 Which executeth judgment for the oppressed; which giveth′ food to the‿hungry.
The′ Lörd looseth the prisoners:
8 The Lord openeth the′ eyes of the‿blind:
The Lord raiseth them that are bowed down: the′ Lörd loveth the righteous:
9 The Lord preserveth the strangers; he relieveth the′ fatherless and widow:
But the way of the wicked he′ turn-eth up-side down.

PSALMS.

10 The LORD shall reign for ever, even thy God, O
    Zion, unto' all gene-rations.
Pr'äise ye the LORD.

PSALM CXLVII.

PRAISE ye the LORD: for it is good to sing praises
    unto our God;
For it is' pleasant; and praise is comely.
2 The LORD doth build' up Je-rusalem:
    He gathereth to'gether the outcasts of Israel.
3 He healeth the' broken in heart,
    And' bind-eth up their wounds.
4 He telleth the' number of the stars;
    He calleth them' äll by their names.
5 Great is our LORD, and of' grëat power:
    His' und-er-standing is infinite.
6 The LORD lifteth' up the meek;
    He casteth the' wicked down to the ground.
7 Sing unto the' LORD with thanksgiving;
    Sing praise upon the' harp un-to our God;
8 Who covereth the heaven with clouds, who
    prepareth' rain for the earth,
Who maketh grass to' grow up-on the mountains.
9 He giveth to the' beast his food,
    And' to the young ravens which cry.
10 He delighteth not in the' strength of the horse:
    He taketh not pleasure' in the legs of a man.
11 The LORD taketh pleasure in' them that fear him,
    In those that' höpe in his mercy.
12 Praise the LORD', O Je-rusalem;
    Pr'aise thy God, O Zion.
13 For he hath strengthened the' bars of thy gates;
    He hath' blessed thy children with-in thee.
14 He maketh' peace in thy borders,
    And filleth thee with the' fin-est of the wheat.

15 He sendeth forth his com′mandment upon earth:
His′ word runneth ve-ry swiftly.
16 He giveth′ snow like wool:
He scattereth the′ höar frost like ashes.
17 He casteth forth his′ ice like morsels:
Who can′ stand be-fore his cold?
18 He sendeth out his′ word, and melteth‿them:
He causeth his wind to blow′, and the wa-ters flow.
19 He showeth his′ word unto Jacob,
His statutes and his′ judg-ments un-to Israel.
20 He hath not dealt so with any nation; and as for
his judgments, they′ have not known‿them.
Pr′äise ye the Lord.

PSALM CXLVIII.

PRAISE′ ye the Lord,
Praise ye the Lord from the heavens′: praise
him in the heights.
2 Praise ye him′, all his angels:
Praise ye him′, ä′ll his hosts.
3 Praise ye him′, sun and moon:
Praise him′, all ye stars of light.
4 Praise him, ye′ heavens of heavens,
And ye waters that′ be a-bove the heavens.
5 Let them praise the′ name of the‿Lord:
For he commanded′, and they were cre-ated.
6 He hath also established them for′ ever and ever:
He hath made a de′cree which shall not pass.
7 Praise the Lord′ from the earth,
Ye′ dragons, and äll deeps:
8 Fire, and hail′; snow, and vapours;
Stormy′ wind ful-filling his word:
9 Mountains, and′ äll hills;
Fruitful′ trëes, and all cedars:
10 Beasts, and′ äll cattle;
Creeping′ things, and fly-ing fowl:

PSALMS.

11 Kings of the earth, and' äll people;
Princes', and all judges of the earth:
12 Both young' men and maidens;
O'''ld men and children:
13 Let them praise the name of the LORD: for his
name a'lone is excellent;
His glory is a'bove the earth and heaven.
14 He also exalteth the horn of his people, the praise
of' all his saints;
Even of the children of Israel, a people near unto
him'. Präise ye the LORD.

PSALM CXLIX.

PRAISE' ye the LORD.
Sing unto the LORD a new song, and his praise
in the' con-gre-gation of saints.
2 Let Israel rejoice in' him that made him:
Let the children of Zion be' joy-ful in their King.
3 Let them praise his' name in the dance:
Let them sing praises unto him' with the timbrel
and harp.
4 For the LORD taketh pleasure' in his people:
He will beautify the' mëek with sal-vation.
5 Let the saints be' joyful in glory:
Let them sing a'loud up-on their beds.
6 Let the high praises of God be' in their mouth,
And a two-edged' swörd in their hand;
7 To execute vengeance up'on the heathen,
And' punishments up-on the people;
8 To bind their' kings with chains,
And their' nobles with fetters of iron;
9 To execute upon them the' judg-ment written:
This honour have all his saints'. Präise ye the
LORD.

PSALM CL.

PRAISE ye the LORD. Praise' God in͜ his sanctuary:
  Praise him in the' firma-ment of his power.
2 Praise him for his' might-y acts:
  Praise him ac'cording to͜ his excel-lent greatness.
3 Praise him with the' sound of the͜ trumpet:
  Praise him' with the psaltery and harp.
4 Praise him with the' timbrel and dance:
  Praise him with' string-ed instruments and organs.
5 Praise him up'on the͜ loud cymbals:
  Praise him up'on the͜ high sound-ing cymbals.
6 Let everything that hath breath' praise the LORD.
  Pr'äise ye the LORD.

———

Glory be to the Father, and' to the Son,
And' to the Ho-ly Ghost:
As it was in the beginning, is now, and' ev-er
  shall͜ be,
World' with-out end. A-men.

THE END.

www.ingramcontent.com/pod-product-compliance
Lightning Source LLC
Chambersburg PA
CBHW020921230426
43666CB00008B/1528